Diet recommendations for nephrotic syndrome

Please check these recommendations always with a nutrition consultant, therapist, doctor or dietician. The recipes and the list of ingredients are supporting the conventional medical therapy. The calorie disclosures of fresh ingredients (fruit and vegetables) vary according to quality and time of harvest. The contents were checked by a dietician and a nutrition consultant for the Traditional Chinese Medicine (TCM).

Author:
©2019 Josef Miligui
www.ebns.at

Source:
The lists are created from the EBNS database for nutritional counseling. The database is used by dietitians, therapists and doctors for advising the patient / client.

Literature:
The specialist literature and the training documents of the German and Austrian dietary and traditional Chinese medicine serve as a knowledge base. We have used the documents as a basis of knowledge, adapted it to our experience and completed them.
http://di-book.com

Production and publishing:
BoD – Books on Demand, Norderstedt
ISBN: 9783746025827

Diet recommendations for DIETETICS - Protein and electrolyte - kidney - Nephrotic syndrome

1   Treatment strategy

Protein-normalized, low-sodium diet.
Liquid intake as instructed by the doctor.
Energy quotient ~ 35 kcal per kg body weight;
Use of high quality greases and oils.

2   Avoid

Heavily salted food.
Biologically low quality protein.

3   Breakfast

4 Snack

5 Lunch

6   Afternoon

7   Dinner

8   Any time

9 Recipes

(rec.) = You can use more.
(little) = You should use less than specified
(omit) = omit.

9.1 Antipasti

Improves blood circulation, anti-inflammatory, relieves pain. Diuretic, promotes digestion, reduces blood pressure, antioxidative, antibacterial, affects anorexia, improves digestion, flatulence, stomach weakness, stimulating.
Cooking time approx. 40 min
1 portion to 740g. / 301kcal. - (carb:0% / prot:0%)
100g.=40,68kcal. / protein 8,24g. fat:16,82g.
µg. - Ph:23,8 Na:3,24 Ka:202,63 Mg:15,42 Ca:21,64 Fe:0,73 Zn:0,24 Col.:0,02 Hsr.:17,4

Quantity of ingredients:
Pepperoni 1 piece / 5g. (yes)
Lemon juice 1 table spoon / 10g. (yes)
Aubergine 1 piece / 300g. (yes)
Tomato 4 pieces / 200g. (yes)
Zucchini 5/8 oz / 200g. (yes)
Lemon peel 1/2 piece / 3g. (yes)
Olive oil 1 table spoon / 15g. (yes)
Basil (fresh) 8 leaves / 5g. (yes)
Salt 1 pinch / 0,5g. (little)
Coriander 1/2 teaspoon / 2g. (yes)

Cooking instructions:
Preheat the oven to 250 degrees Celsius and bake the hot peppers until the bowl becomes dark (about 20 minutes). Cover the hot peppers with a clear film and allow to cool. Peel the skin and cut into strips about 2 cm wide. Cut tomatoes in half and spread with oil in slices of aubergine and bake in the oven at 200 degrees golden brown (about 10 minutes) Fry the zucchini slices in the grill pan (without fat).
Mix everything together, mix the marinade of olive oil, salt and lemon peel and pour over the vegetables, sprinkle with coriander. Leave for 1 hour.

9.2 Apple - banana cream

Regulates gastrointestinal function, provides vitamin C, cholesterol lowering, reduces inflammation, diuretic, improves

blood circulation.
Cooking time approx. 15 min
4 portions to 206,25g. / 113kcal. - (carb:0% / prot:0%)
100g.=54,79kcal. / protein 0,84g. fat:0,51g.
µg. - Ph:3,01 Na:0,49 Ka:38,02 Mg:2,73 Ca:2,25 Fe:0,1 Zn:0,03 Col.:0 Hsr.:3,19

Quantity of ingredients:
Apple (sour) 7/8 lbs / 400g. (yes)
Water 3/4 cup - 6 oz / 200g. (yes)
Orange peel 1/4 piece / 5g. (yes)
Lemon peel 1/2 piece / 2g. (yes)
Sugar brown 2 teaspoons / 6g. (yes)
Cinnamon sticks 1 piece / 0g. (yes)
Banana 1 piece / 150g. (yes)
Acerola fruit nectar or powder 1 teaspoon / 2g. (yes)
Orange juice 1/2 piece / 50g. (yes)
Lemon juice 1 table spoon / 10g. (yes)

Cooking instructions:
Cut the apple into fine slices, bring water to boil and add the apple slices, orange- and lemon peel, sugar and cinnamon and simmer about 7 minutes. The apples should be almost soft. Remove acerola and the cinnamon stick. Mix the apple, the banana, the orange juice and the lemon juice.

9.3 Apricot and cranberry ice cream

Forces resistance to infections, good to fight oral mucosal inflammation, diarrhea. Has a positive effect on the urinary tract.
Cooking time approx. 5 min
2 portions to 222,5g. / 106kcal. - (carb:91% / prot:9%)
100g.=47,87kcal. / protein 1,9g. fat:0,48g.
µg. - Ph:7,98 Na:0,94 Ka:107,17 Mg:4,69 Ca:8,02 Fe:0,03 Zn:0 Col.:0 Hsr.:8,57

Quantity of ingredients:
Apricots 3/4 lbs / 350g. (yes)
Water 1/4 cup / 50g. (yes)
Cranberry 3 table spoons / 45g. (yes)

Cooking instructions:
Mix the apricot juice with the cranberry syrup. Fill the juice into little molds, place in the freezer and let it freeze in about 3 hours.

9.4   Avocado with lemon

Good to fight insomnia, inflammation, swelling, pain and itching. Is calming.
Cooking time approx. 5 min
1 portion to 131g. / 289kcal. - (carb:17% / prot:83%)
100g.=220,61kcal. / protein 2,34g. fat:28,24g.
µg. - Ph:37,02 Na:5,86 Ka:469,27 Mg:29,31 Ca:11,83 Fe:0,59 Zn:0,37 Col.:0 Hsr.:29,01

Quantity of ingredients:
Avocado 1/2 piece / 120g. (yes)
Lemon juice 1/2 piece / 10g. (yes)
Salt 1 pinch / 1g. (little)

Cooking instructions:
Halve the avocado, remove the core, add the lemon juice, salt a little and eat with a spoon.

9.5   Banana Soymilk

Good to fight loss of appetite, oral mucosa inflammation. Strengthens body energy, promotes stomach-spleen harmony, promotes digestion, regulates gastrointestinal function. Relieves pain, detoxifying, bactericide.
Cooking time approx. 5 min
Allergens: E
2 portions to 263g. / 126kcal. - (carb:0% / prot:0%)
100g.=47,72kcal. / protein 7,49g. fat:4,13g.
µg. - Ph:21,94 Na:251,11 Ka:110,08 Mg:13,31 Ca:9,78 Fe:0,4 Zn:0,21 Col.:0 Hsr.:33,68

Quantity of ingredients:
Banana 1 piece / 120g. (yes)
Soybean milk 1 1/2 cups / 400g. (little)
Honey 1 teaspoon / 3g. (yes)
Cinnamon ground 1 pinch / 1g. (yes)
Acerola fruit nectar or powder 1 teaspoon / 2g. (yes)

Cooking instructions:
Cut the banana into pieces, puree them with soy milk, acerola, honey and cinnamon with the mixing stick.

9.6   Barley mash with steamed pear

Promotes digestion, supports urination, promotes spleen, diuretic, forcing spleen, relaxes, promotes perspiration.

Cooking time approx. 25 min
Allergens: A
5 portions to 305,8g. / 114kcal. - (carb:86% / prot:14%)
100g.=37,21kcal. / protein 3,26g. fat:0,72g.
µg. - Ph:1,16 Na:0,11 Ka:2,09 Mg:0,44 Ca:0,33 Fe:0,01 Zn:0,01 Col.:0 Hsr.:0,42

Quantity of ingredients:
Water 10 cups / 1200g. (yes)
Barley 1 cup / 120g. (yes)
Ginger fresh 2 slices / 2g. (yes)
Cardamom 3 capsules / 1g. (yes)
Salt 1 pinch / 1g. (little)
Pear 1 piece / 200g. (yes)
Sugar cane sugar 1/2 teaspoon / 5g. (yes)

Cooking instructions:
Grind coarse the barley and roast it dry. Add hot water, add ginger and cardamom and let it swell to a pulp in low heat. Peel and dice the pear and boil for 10 minutes with a little water. At the end, add the stewed pear, a little butter and sweetener.

Variant: If you want to go fast, you can use barley flakes instead of shot.

9.7   Basic recipe for a chicken broth worming

Strengthens blood, strengthens bone marrow, reduces blood pressure, strengthens immune system, prevents cancer, reduces radiation damage, promotes sweating, dissolves stagnation, good to fight loss of appetite, flatulence.
Cooking time approx. 2-3 hours
Allergens: L
9 portions to 244,89g. / 90kcal. - (carb:10% / prot:90%)
100g.=36,66kcal. / protein 15,68g. fat:11,56g.
µg. - Ph:0,86 Na:0,59 Ka:1,87 Mg:0,13 Ca:0,38 Fe:0,01 Zn:0 Col.:0,25 Hsr.:0,92

Quantity of ingredients:
Chicken meat 1/2 piece / 600g. (little)
Carrot 2 pieces / 150g. (yes)
Leek 1 stick / 45g. (yes)
Celery root 1 piece / 500g. (yes)
Ginger fresh 2 slices / 2g. (yes)
Fenugreek (Trigonella foenum-graecum) 1 teaspoon / 2g. (yes)
Juniper berry 1 teaspoon / 3g. (yes)
Bay leaf 3 pieces / 2g. (yes)

Water 4 cup / 900g. (yes)

Cooking instructions:
Remove chicken parts from fat. Place chicken pieces in a saucepan with hot water and heat till it boils briefly, skimming any resulting foam. Add coarsely chopped vegetables and all spices and cook over medium heat for 2 to 3 hours. Strain the finished soup. Throw away vegetables and bones.
Tip: If you want to use the meat as a soup insert, take out after 45 minutes and return only the bones in the soup.
Refrigerate for later use.

9.8 Basic recipe for a reissue soup (Congee)

Low fat content, for the drainage of the body overweight and high blood pressure.
Cooking time approx. 2-4 hours
3 portions to 273,33g. / 140kcal. - (carb:90% / prot:10%)
100g.=51,34kcal. / protein 2,96g. fat:0,48g.
µg. - Ph:1,95 Na:0,19 Ka:1,67 Mg:1,14 Ca:0,57 Fe:0,01 Zn:0,02 Col.:0 Hsr.:2,11

Quantity of ingredients:
Rice variety any 1 cup / 120g. (yes)
Water 6 cups / 700g. (yes)

Cooking instructions:
Cook rice and water in a ratio of about 1: 6. The amount of water determines the thickness of the mash (matter of taste).
Put the rice in a saucepan with a heavy lid. It is important to simmer the rice after a short boil on the slightest flame, otherwise it burns.
Boil the rice for 2-4 hours. The longer it cooks, the more it strengthens. If you want to eat the dish for breakfast, you can put the rice on just before bedtime.
To be on the safe side, you should first check the behavior of your pot and cooker under observation for a similar amount of time, so that nothing burns.
Refrigerate for later use.

9.9 Basic recipe for a vegetable soup, nutritious

Reduces blood pressure, strengthens immune system, prevents cancer, forcing spleen, dissolves stagnation, promotes weight loss. Good to fight immunodeficiency, high blood pressure, depressions, diabetes, diarrhea, reduces blood lipids.

Cooking time approx. 2-3 hours
Allergens: L
5 portions to 240,6g. / 48kcal. - (carb:0% / prot:0%)
100g.=19,87kcal. / protein 1,56g. fat:1,31g.
µg. - Ph:4,86 Na:3,67 Ka:25,68 Mg:1,8 Ca:6,32 Fe:0,1 Zn:0,05 Col.:0 Hsr.:2,78

Quantity of ingredients:
Olive oil 1 table spoon / 4g. (yes)
Onion white 1 piece / 60g. (yes)
Carrot 3 pieces / 200g. (yes)
Parsnip 3/8 lbs - 6oz / 150g. (yes)
Celery root 1 cup / 100g. (yes)
Ginger fresh 1/2 teaspoon / 2g. (yes)
Lemon 1/2 piece / 25g. (yes)
Juniper berry 6 pieces / 6g. (yes)
Thyme dried 1 pinch / 1g. (yes)
Lovage 1 table spoon / 3g. (yes)
Bay leaf 2 leaves / 1g. (yes)
Salt 1 pinch / 1g. (little)
Water 3 cups / 650g. (yes)

Cooking instructions:
Cut the vegetables into cubes.
Heat oil in hot pot, fry shortly onions and vegetables.
Add cold water, then add ginger, bay leaf and lemon juice.
Season with juniper, thyme and lovage. Cover for 2 - 3 hours on a low heat and simmer.
The used vegetables should be thrown away.
The basic recipe serves as a soup base and to refine vegetables, legumes or cereals.
If you want to eat vegetable soup immediately, add the desired vegetables half an hour before.
Refrigerate for later use.

9.10 Bitter lemon drink

Appetizing
Cooking time approx. 5 min
1 portion to 250g. / 130kcal. - (carb:93% / prot:7%)
100g.=52kcal. / protein 2,5g. fat:0g.
µg. - Ph:6 Na:4 Ka:1 Mg:1 Ca:4 Fe:0 Zn:0 Col.:0 Hsr.:0

Quantity of ingredients:
Bitter Lemon 1 cup / 250g. (yes)

9.11 Boiled celery salad with exotic spices

Forcing spleen, relieves diarrhea, antibacterial, blood-forming, blood detoxifying, reduces inflammation, diuretic, improves blood circulation.
Cooking time approx. 30 min
Allergens: GLMNO
4 portions to 341g. / 166kcal. - (carb:48% / prot:52%)
100g.=48,61kcal. / protein 5,59g. fat:9,17g.
µg. - Ph:3,39 Na:6,17 Ka:17,47 Mg:0,76 Ca:5,05 Fe:0,03 Zn:0,01 Col.:0,2 Hsr.:3,02

Quantity of ingredients:
Celery root 1 1/2 piece / 900g. (yes)
Yogurt (natural, 3.5% fat) 1 cup / 250g. (yes)
Sour cream 15% fat 2 table spoons / 20g. (little)
Turmeric (yellow root) 1 pinch / 1g. (yes)
Sesame oil 1 table spoon / 20g. (yes)
Pepper (ground) 1 pinch / 0,5g. ()
Lemongrass 1 pinch / 1g. (yes)
Onion white 1/2 piece / 25g. (yes)
Mustard 1/2 teaspoon / 1g. (yes)
Black caraway 1 pinch / 1g. (yes)
Salt 1 pinch / 1g. (little)
Lemon juice 1 piece / 40g. (yes)
Apple (sour) 1/2 piece / 100g. (yes)
Peppers powder 1 pinch / 1g. (yes)
Vinegar (Apple vinegar) 1 dash / 3g. (yes)

Cooking instructions:
Cook the peeled celeriac in thick slices and then cut into bite-sized strips.

Dressing: Mix a little yoghurt, sour cream, turmeric, sesame oil, pepper, lemongrass powder, finely chopped onion, a little mustard, salt, crushed black cumin, some cold water, lemon juice or vinegar; add the sour chopped apple, some rose paprika, the lukewarm celery and mix well; let it rest for 2 - 3 hours or overnight.

Ideal as a substitute for raw food

9.12 Breakfast - low protein

Increase appetite, detoxifying, increases blood glucose levels,

harmonizes heart rhythm, good to fight vomiting, nutritional disorders, diarrhea.
Cooking time approx. 10 min
Allergens: GO
1 portion to 330g. / 575kcal. - (carb:69% / prot:31%)
100g.=174,24kcal. / protein 4,87g. fat:27,83g.
µg. - Ph:104,21 Na:225,52 Ka:58,03 Mg:6,12 Ca:26,88 Fe:0,27 Zn:0,23 Col.:15,74
Hsr.:47,27

Quantity of ingredients:
Bread with carob kernel flour 3 oz / 80g. (yes)
Butter organic 1/2 oz / 20g. (little)
Apricot jam 1 oz / 30g. (yes)
Fresh cheese with herbs 1 oz / 30g. (little)
Coffee 1/2 cup / 150g. (little)
Sugar white 1/2 oz / 10g. (yes)

Cooking instructions:
Prepare coffee to taste, make fresh cheese if possible with fresh herbs yourself.

9.13 Breakfast - Rice with fruits

Good to fight blood circulation disorders, thrombose, risk of embolism, high blood pressure, a headache, heart attack and stroke. Encourages blood build-up, promotes digestion, reduces Inflammation.
Cooking time approx. 10 min - 3 hours
Allergens: GHO
3 portions to 282g. / 231kcal. - (carb:90% / prot:10%)
100g.=81,8kcal. / protein 3,59g. fat:7,61g.
µg. - Ph:3,19 Na:0,7 Ka:8,57 Mg:20,72 Ca:21,22 Fe:0,05 Zn:0,02 Col.:0,54 Hsr.:0,92

Quantity of ingredients:
Basic recipe for a rice soup (Congee) 6 cups / 500g. (yes)
Cow's milk (whole milk 3.5% fat) 1/2 to 1 cup / 80g. (yes)
Honey 1 table spoon / 10g. (yes)
Butter organic 1 table spoon / 15g. (little)
Dates dried 1 table spoon / 15g. (yes)
Fig 1 table spoon / 15g. (yes)
Apple (sour) 1 piece / 200g. (yes)
Hazelnuts 1/2 teaspoon / 5g. (yes)
Almond 1/2 teaspoon / 5g. (yes)
Cinnamon ground 1 pinch / 1g. (yes)

Cooking instructions:

Cook rice congee according to basic recipe or use pre-cooked.
Make it with the milk more fluid, and sweet with honey.
Fry the fruits and nuts in butter and mix with the finished rice soup, add chopped dates, figs and the apple.

9.14 Carrot and potato rucola sandwich

Reduces inflammation, improves digestion, supports urination, lowers cholesterol, strengthens immune system, prevents cancer, good to fight constipation (Fibre-rich), dissolves stagnation.
Cooking time approx. 20 min
Allergens: AG
4 portions to 116,25g. / 94kcal. - (carb:55% / prot:45%)
100g.=80,86kcal. / protein 2,68g. fat:2,83g.
µg. - Ph:4,15 Na:4,56 Ka:16,7 Mg:1,23 Ca:1,78 Fe:0,06 Zn:0,03 Col.:0,25 Hsr.:1,27

Quantity of ingredients:
Carrot 1 piece / 50g. (yes)
Sour cream 15% fat 3 table spoons / 45g. (little)
Onion (spring onion) 1 piece / 20g. (yes)
Rucola 1/2 bunch / 100g. ()
Lemon peel 1/4 teaspoon / 1g. (yes)
Salt 1 pinch / 1g. (little)
Pepper (ground) 1 pinch / 0,2g. ()
Whole grain bread 8 slices / 48g. (yes)

Cooking instructions:
Cook the potatoes gently, peel and squeeze through the potato press.
Cook vegetable broth according to the basic recipe and remove a carrot after a short cooking time and finely crush with a fork.
Stir the potatoes, carrots, grated lemon zest and sour cream into a smooth cream.
Mix carrot and potato cream with finely chopped rocket salad. Season the spread with salt and pepper and spread the bread. Sprinkle with the finely chopped young onions.

9.15 Carrot and rice gruel soup

Stops diarrhea, good to fight fever, strengthens immune system, reduces blood pressure.
Cooking time approx. 10 min
1 portion to 224g. / 101kcal. - (carb:96% / prot:4%)
100g.=45,09kcal. / protein 2,37g. fat:0,4g.
µg. - Ph:27,48 Na:20,34 Ka:65,63 Mg:170,89 Ca:178,57 Fe:1,03 Zn:0,34 Col.:0 Hsr.:12,3

Quantity of ingredients:
Basic recipe for a rice soup (Congee) 1 cup / 120g. (yes)
Carrot 2 pieces / 100g. (yes)
Salt 1 teaspoon / 4g. (little)

Cooking instructions:
Peel and grate carrots. Heat the rice soup (according to the basic recipe) till it boils and add the grated carrots and salt. Cook for 10 minutes.

9.16 Carrot drink

Promotes spleen and liver, reduces blood pressure, strengthens immune system, prevents cancer, reduces radiation damage, diuretic, building up, eye-enhancing, detoxifying, nerve-strengthening.
Cooking time approx. 15 min
Allergens: H
1 portion to 265g. / 143kcal. - (carb:81% / prot:19%)
100g.=53,96kcal. / protein 3,78g. fat:2,5g.
µg. - Ph:43,4 Na:22,3 Ka:117,79 Mg:18,2 Ca:36,26 Fe:1,83 Zn:0,55 Col.:0 Hsr.:17,98

Quantity of ingredients:
Millet flakes 1 table spoon / 10g. (yes)
Carrot 7/8 lbs / 200g. (yes)
Almond puree 1 teaspoon / 3g. (yes)
Honey 1/2 teaspoon / 2g. (yes)
Water 1/4 cup / 50g. (yes)

Cooking instructions:
Sprinkle millet flakes with 50 ml of cold water and let it swell for 10 minutes.
Juice the fresh carrots or use 200 ml. carrot juice.
Puree the millet flakes, carrot juice, almond paste and honey with the blender.

9.17 Celery and potato cream soup

Reduces blood pressure, strengthens immune system, promotes weight loss. Good to fight immunodeficiency, loss of appetite, flatulence, depressions, diabetes, diarrhea, improves digestion.
Cooking time approx. 45 min
Allergens: GL
4 portions to 241,5g. / 113kcal. - (carb:83% / prot:17%)
100g.=46,69kcal. / protein 2,15g. fat:5,52g.
µg. - Ph:5,96 Na:3,46 Ka:23,98 Mg:22,27 Ca:83,51 Fe:0,18 Zn:0,01 Col.:0 Hsr.:1,49

Quantity of ingredients:
Olive oil 1 table spoon / 10g. (yes)
Onion white 1/2 piece / 25g. (yes)
Basic recipe for a vegetable soup (nutritious) 3 cups / 700g. (yes)
Nutmeg 1 pinch / 0,5g. (yes)
Ground 1 pinch / 0,5g. (yes)
Lemon peel 1/4 piece / 1g. (yes)
Crème fraiche cheese 2 table spoons / 20g. (little)
Salt 1 pinch / 1g. (little)
Parsley 1 table spoon / 8g. (yes)

Cooking instructions:
Heat the olive oil in a saucepan lightly. Fry the onions very gently in a mild heat. Pour with vegetable stock according to the basic recipe. Cover and cook for 15 minutes.
Add curd-cut potato, celery, nutmeg, cumin and lemon zest. Spice with salt and cook for 12 minutes. Potatoes and celery should be soft. Remove the lemon peel.
Puree the soup with crème fraiche using a blender. Season the soup with salt.
Arrange the soup in portions with the chopped parsley.

9.18 Celery soup

Forcing spleen, calms nerves, stimulates appetite and digestion, dissolves stagnation.
Cooking time approx. 45 min
Allergens: ACGL
4 portions to 285,5g. / 101kcal. - (carb:44% / prot:56%)
100g.=35,38kcal. / protein 4,32g. fat:5,7g.
µg. - Ph:2,76 Na:5,05 Ka:11,06 Mg:0,62 Ca:2,85 Fe:0,03 Zn:0,01 Col.:1,44 Hsr.:2,12

Quantity of ingredients:
Water 2 cup / 500g. (yes)
Butter organic 1 table spoon / 15g. (little)
Nutmeg 1 pinch / 1g. (yes)
Salt 1 pinch / 1g. (little)
Spelled wholemeal flour 2-3 teaspoons / 25g. (yes)
Celery root 1 piece / 500g. (yes)
Chicken egg 1 piece / 55g. (little)
Cream sour 10% 2 table spoons / 25g. (little)
Celery sticks 2 table spoons / 20g. (yes)
Pepper (ground) 1 pinch / 0,5g. ()

Cooking instructions:
In a hot saucepan, melt 1 tbsp butter; add a pinch of nutmeg, a pinch of salt, 1/2 cup wholegrain spelled flour (finely ground as fresh as possible) and stir to a sweat while stirring; add 1/2 liter of hot water gradually; add 1 large finely chopped celery tuber; cook for about 35 minutes and then puree; mix 1 egg yolk with 1 cup of cream; in the hot - no longer boiling! - soup vigorously; add some celery leaves finely chopped; with pepper, salt to taste.

9.19 Champignon salad with cress

Promotes digestion and is good to fight high blood pressure. Good to fight loss of appetite, improves blood circulation.
Cooking time approx. 5 min
Allergens: AN
1 portion to 312g. / 220kcal. - (carb:56% / prot:44%)
100g.=70,51kcal. / protein 9,74g. fat:7,08g.
µg. - Ph:105,24 Na:37,35 Ka:366,67 Mg:14,25 Ca:19,03 Fe:1,08 Zn:0,41 Col.:0,02
Hsr.:60,22

Quantity of ingredients:
Champignon 5/8 lbs - 8oz / 250g. (yes)
Sesame oil 2 table spoons / 6g. (yes)
Pepper (ground) 1 pinch / 0,5g. ()
Salt 1 pinch / 1g. (little)
Lemon 1/2 piece / 15g. (yes)
Peppers powder 2 pinches / 0,1g. (yes)
Cress 2 table spoons / 10g. (yes)
White bread (wheat bread) 2 slices / 30g. (yes)

Cooking instructions:
Cut mushrooms into thin slices.
Dressing: sesame oil, a little ground pepper, salt, plenty of lemon juice, stir well the rose pepper; give over the finely chopped mushrooms; plenty of watercress.
Goes well with: white bread, round grain rice or quinoa; Along with the cereal, the salad makes a simple, light meal.
Serve with white bread.

9.20 Chicken soup with egg yolk and parsley

Strengthens blood, strengthens bone marrow, reduces blood pressure, strengthens immune system. Parsley stimulates liver function,

harmonizes liver and spleen, strengthens eyesight, detoxifying.
Cooking time approx. 10 min
Allergens: CL
2 portions to 260g. / 118kcal. - (carb:82% / prot:18%)
100g.=45,19kcal. / protein 16,35g. fat:2,49g.
µg. - Ph:6,98 Na:8,83 Ka:9 Mg:24,79 Ca:69,4 Fe:0,28 Zn:0,05 Col.:6,52 Hsr.:2,22

Quantity of ingredients:
Basic recipe for a chicken soup (warming) 2 cup / 500g. (yes)
Chicken yolk 1 piece / 10g. (little)
Parsley 1 table spoon / 10g. (yes)

Cooking instructions:
Cook the chicken broth according to the basic recipe.
Heat broth and bubble the egg yolk. Sprinkle the chopped parsley over
it and let it rest for about 2 minutes. Drink in small sips.

9.21 Chicory salad with tangerine

Dissolves mucus, is rich in A-B-C Vitamins, promotes digestion, forcing
spleen, promotes weight loss. Good to fight loss
of appetite, flatulence, immunodeficiency.
Cooking time approx. 10 min
Allergens: AGNO
3 portions to 285g. / 257kcal. - (carb:75% / prot:25%)
100g.=90,06kcal. / protein 5,49g. fat:7,73g.
µg. - Ph:8,6 Na:15,26 Ka:56,29 Mg:4 Ca:9,42 Fe:0,13 Zn:0,04 Col.:0,01 Hsr.:7,09

Quantity of ingredients:
Tangerine 4 pieces / 300g. (yes)
Chicory 2-3 pieces / 300g. (yes)
Sesame oil 2 table spoons / 18g. (yes)
Pepper (ground) 1 pinch / 0,5g. ()
Salt 1 pinch / 1g. (little)
Vinegar Aceto Balsamico 2 teaspoons / 6g. (yes)
Lemon 1/2 piece / 25g. (yes)
Orange 1/2 piece / 70g. (yes)
Peppers powder 1 pinch / 1g. (yes)
Orange jam 1 teaspoon / 4g. (yes)
Cream, sweet 30% 1 table spoon / 10g. (little)
White bread (wheat bread) 6 slices / 120g. (yes)

Cooking instructions:
Peel tangerines and cut into bite-sized pieces; Cut chicory roughly and

mix well.
Dressing: sesame oil, pepper, salt, raspberry vinegar or balsamic vinegar, a little lemon or orange juice, rose paprika, orange marmalade or, alternatively, another jam, stir well. Give a little sweet cream over the salad and let it pass briefly.

9.22 Coffee

Supports urination, stimulates appetite, detoxifying, increases blood glucose levels, harmonizes heart rhythm.
Cooking time approx. 5 min
1 portion to 129g. / 16kcal. - (carb:100% / prot:0%)
100g.=12,4kcal. / protein 0,01g. fat:0g.
µg. - Ph:0,08 Na:0,97 Ka:2,62 Mg:1,16 Ca:4,76 Fe:0,02 Zn:0,09 Col.:0 Hsr.:3,91

Quantity of ingredients:
Coffee 1 table spoon / 5g. (little)
Water 1 cup / 120g. (yes)
Sugar white 1 teaspoon / 4g. (yes)

Cooking instructions:
Depending on your taste, prepare a filter coffee, espresso or "Turkish".

9.23 Cola drink

Good to fight lack of appetite, changed sense of taste.
Cooking time approx. 1 min
1 portion to 250g. / 150kcal. - (carb:76% / prot:24%)
100g.=60kcal. / protein 8,25g. fat:0g.
µg. - Ph:6 Na:4 Ka:1 Mg:1 Ca:4 Fe:0 Zn:0 Col.:0 Hsr.:10

Quantity of ingredients:
Cola drink 1 cup / 250g. (yes)

9.24 Compote from plums

Cancer preventive effect, dehydrates the body, stimulates digestion and binds fats in the intestine.
Cooking time approx. 10 min
2 portions to 170,5g. / 22kcal. - (carb:93% / prot:7%)
100g.=13,2kcal. / protein 0,32g. fat:0,06g.
µg. - Ph:1,73 Na:0,34 Ka:17,94 Mg:0,8 Ca:2,7 Fe:0,03 Zn:0,02 Col.:0 Hsr.:1,47

Quantity of ingredients:
Plums 1/4 lbs - 4oz / 100g. (yes)

Water 1 1/2 cups / 240g. (yes)
Cinnamon ground 1 pinch / 1g. (yes)

Cooking instructions:
Boil plums in water until soft. Sprinkle with a little cinnamon.

9.25 Compote of pears

Pear benefits digestion, supports urination. Cocoa forces liver,
strengthens the muscles, strengthens the defense. Good
to fight fungi infections.
Cooking time approx. 10 min
4 portions to 270,75g. / 122kcal. - (carb:93% / prot:7%)
100g.=45,24kcal. / protein 1,27g. fat:0,86g.
µg. - Ph:0,76 Na:0,11 Ka:6,01 Mg:0,38 Ca:0,62 Fe:0,01 Zn:0,01 Col.:0 Hsr.:0,69

Quantity of ingredients:
Water 1 cup / 280g. (yes)
Pear 4 pieces / 800g. (yes)
Anise (Common Fennel) 1/2 teaspoon / 1g. (yes)
Vanilla pod 1 pinch / 1g. (yes)
Chili (pod or ground) very little / 0,2g. (yes)
Cocoa 1 pinch / 1g. (yes)

Cooking instructions:
Boil pears (organic - with peel), aniseed, vanilla, chili soft. Sprinkle with
cocoa.

9.26 Corn coffee with cardamom

Diuretic, forcing spleen, supports urination, relaxes, reduces fat.
Cooking time approx. 5 min
1 portion to 136g. / 3kcal. - (carb:99% / prot:1%)
100g.=2,21kcal. / protein 0,11g. fat:0,08g.
µg. - Ph:1,29 Na:1,02 Ka:7,9 Mg:2,49 Ca:5,37 Fe:0,08 Zn:0,09 Col.:0 Hsr.:0

Quantity of ingredients:
Cereal coffee 1 table spoon / 15g. (yes)
Cardamom 2 cores / 1g. (yes)
Water 1 cup / 120g. (yes)

Cooking instructions:
Boil water, coffee, sugar and cardamom. Let it set for one min before
drinking.

9.27 Cranberry yogurt mix

Good to fight acute or chronic constipation of the intestine, oral mucosal inflammation, diarrhea, flatulence, throat irritation.
Cooking time approx. 5 min
Allergens: GO
2 portions to 197,5g. / 57kcal. - (carb:75% / prot:25%)
100g.=28,86kcal. / protein 2,13g. fat:1,02g.
µg. - Ph:7,17 Na:5,87 Ka:13,16 Mg:2,71 Ca:16,61 Fe:0,01 Zn:0,03 Col.:0,39 Hsr.:0,2

Quantity of ingredients:
Yogurt (natural, 1.5% fat) 1/4 lbs - 4oz / 125g. (yes)
Cranberry jam 2 table spoons / 20g. (yes)
Mineral water 1 cup / 250g. (little)

Cooking instructions:
Mix yoghurt, cranberry jam and mineral water until frothy.

9.28 Cucumber soup

Diuretic, detoxifying, suppresses conversion of sugar into fat, lowers cholesterol, prevents cancer, promotes digestion, diaphoretic, dries out, good to fight yeast infections.
Cooking time approx. 20 min
Allergens: M
4 portions to 235,25g. / 96kcal. - (carb:22% / prot:78%)
100g.=40,6kcal. / protein 0,91g. fat:9,03g.
µg. - Ph:2,67 Na:1,28 Ka:15,6 Mg:1,17 Ca:2,57 Fe:0,06 Zn:0,01 Col.:0 Hsr.:0,85

Quantity of ingredients:
Olive oil 2 table spoons / 35g. (yes)
Cucumber 2 pieces / 400g. (yes)
Water 2 cup / 500g. (yes)
Sage 3 leaves / 3g. (yes)
Mustard 1/2 teaspoon / 0,5g. (yes)
Coriander 1 pinch / 1g. (yes)
Cardamom 1 pinch / 1g. (yes)
Salt 1 pinch / 1g. (little)

Cooking instructions:
Heat oil and roast short the small cucumbers. Add Mustard seeds, coriander, cardamom and salt. Add water. Simmer for 10-15 min. Puree and decorate with fresh chopped sage.

9.29 Delicately spiced zucchini with tomatoes

Diuretic, promotes digestion, helps to digest fat, reduces blood pressure, dissolves stagnation, antioxidative, supports urination, diuretic, warming the body from the inside, expands blood vessels.
Cooking time approx. 10 min
4 portions to 396,5g. / 203kcal. - (carb:72% / prot:28%)
100g.=51,2kcal. / protein 5,38g. fat:6,62g.
µg. - Ph:10,4 Na:0,79 Ka:35,33 Mg:6,3 Ca:5,58 Fe:0,26 Zn:0,02 Col.:0 Hsr.:5,53

Quantity of ingredients:
Olive oil 1 table spoon / 20g. (yes)
Onion white 2 pieces / 120g. (yes)
Zucchini 4 pieces / 800g. (yes)
Oregano dried 1 pinch / 1g. (yes)
Basil (fresh) 6-8 leaves / 3g. (yes)
Salt 1 pinch / 1g. (little)
Tomato 2 pieces / 120g. (yes)
Rice (whole grain) 1 cup / 120g. (yes)
Water 6 cups / 400g. (yes)
Salt 1 pinch / 1g. (little)

Cooking instructions:
In a hot pan, fry olive oil, finely chopped onions and finely chopped zucchini until half cooked. Add plenty of dried oregano. Salt and chop the tomatoes for a few minutes until the zucchini are tender but crisp. Add fresh basil as desired.

Variation: Put some sheep's cheese over the tomatoes and finish cooking with the lid closed.

Place the rice in salted water, heat till it boils and let it simmer over low heat for about 15 minutes.

9.30 Fast polenta with avocado and spring onion

Good to fight inflammations, swelling, pain. Forcing spleen and stomach, lets urine and bile juice flow, dissolves stagnation. Includes unsaturated fatty acids, antioxidative.
Cooking time approx. 10 min
2 portions to 286g. / 450kcal. - (carb:55% / prot:45%)
100g.=157,17kcal. / protein 6,92g. fat:27,5g.
µg. - Ph:16,92 Na:0,99 Ka:54,42 Mg:8,7 Ca:3,02 Fe:0,13 Zn:0,17 Col.:0,01 Hsr.:3,78

Quantity of ingredients:

Corn (fast polenta) 1 cup / 120g. (yes)
Water 1 1/2 cups / 240g. (yes)
Olive oil 1 table spoon / 15g. (yes)
Salt 1 pinch / 1g. (little)
Pepper (ground) 1 pinch / 0,5g. ()
Lemon juice 1 dash / 3g. (yes)
Onion (spring onion) 2 pieces / 40g. (yes)
Avocado 1/2 piece / 150g. (yes)
Turmeric (yellow root) 1 pinch / 1g. (yes)
Basil (fresh) 1 teaspoon / 2g. (yes)

Cooking instructions:
Heat water, add oil, lemon and spices.
When the water boils, add the polenta while stirring constantly and cook for 2 minutes.
When the porridge becomes firm, the polenta is ready.
Add diced avocado and sliced spring onion to the polenta. Sprinkle fresh basil on it.

9.31 Fennel and potato gratin

Reduces inflammation, improves blood circulation, improves digestion, supports urination, lowers cholesterol, good to fight loss of appetite, flatulence, inflammatory bowel disease, heartburn. Forcing spleen, improves blood circulation.
Cooking time approx. 1 1/2 hours
Allergens: CGL
2 portions to 230,5g. / 147kcal. - (carb:68% / prot:32%)
100g.=63,77kcal. / protein 5,72g. fat:5,42g.
µg. - Ph:15 Na:12,98 Ka:80,91 Mg:13,52 Ca:40,41 Fe:0,41 Zn:0,09 Col.:7,81 Hsr.:3,64

Quantity of ingredients:
Fennel 5/8 oz / 200g. (yes)
Potato 1/4 lbs - 4oz / 125g. (rec.)
Basic recipe for a vegetable soup (nutritious) 1/2 cup / 100g. (yes)
Butter organic 1 teaspoon / 3g. (little)
Rice flour 2 teaspoons / 6g. (little)
Cream sour 10% 1 teaspoon / 3g. (little)
Salt 1 pinch / 1g. (little)
Sugar cane sugar 1 pinch / 1g. (yes)
Chicken yolk 1 piece / 10g. (little)
Pepper Cayenne 1 pinch / 0,5g. (yes)
Nutmeg 1 pinch / 0,5g. (yes)
Parsley 1 teaspoon / 2g. (yes)

Chives 1 teaspoon / 3g. (yes)
Parmesan 1 teaspoon / 3g. (little)
Butter organic 1 teaspoon / 3g. (little)

Cooking instructions:
Cook peeled potatoes and then let cool. Wash the fennel, cut off the stems and remove any outer leaves.
Hold back fennel greens and add it to the sauce with the other herbs later.
Steam the fennel tubers for about 15 - 20 minutes.
Then cut the potatoes and fennel into slices and place in layers in a greased baking dish.
Bring the liquid of fennel broth to the boil and bind it with flour.
Season with sea salt, cayenne pepper, sugar, nutmeg and sour cream. Allow to cool and alloy with egg yolk.
Spread the sauce over the casserole, sprinkle with parmesan and finely chopped parsley and chives. Bake at 200 °C / 392 °F in the oven for half an hour.

9.32 Fish soup with rosemary

Promotes spleen and liver, reduces blood pressure, strengthens immune system, prevents cancer, reduces radiation damage, has little cholesterol and is protein rich, improves blood circulation, increases appetite. Antioxidant, forcing spleen, dissolves stagnation.
Cooking time approx. 30 min
Allergens: DLO
4 portions to 284,25g. / 271kcal. - (carb:38% / prot:62%)
100g.=95,43kcal. / protein 15,39g. fat:14,78g.
µg. - Ph:4,93 Na:1,8 Ka:11,89 Mg:0,76 Ca:1,33 Fe:0,03 Zn:0,03 Col.:0,01 Hsr.:3,59

Quantity of ingredients:
Basic recipe for a fish soup 2 cup / 500g. (yes)
Rosemary 1/2 bunch / 7g. (yes)
Onion (spring onion) 1 piece / 20g. (yes)
Olive oil 2 table spoons / 35g. (yes)
Fish pieces mixed (fresh water) 5/8 lbs - 8oz / 250g. (little)
Carrot 1 piece / 120g. (yes)
Parsnip 1 piece / 180g. (yes)
Celery root 1 slice / 20g. (yes)
Salt 1 pinch / 1g. (little)
Peppercorns 2 pieces / 1g. (yes)
Garlic 1 clove / 3g. (yes)

Cooking instructions:
Fry the onion and garlic in oil. Add fish broth. Add diced carrots, parsnips and celery. Season with salt and peppercorns. Simmer the soup on a low heat for 25 minutes.
Wash the fish, drizzle with lemon juice, divide into pieces and add to the soup with the pink rosemary. Cook for 5 min on low heat.
Add the chives and parsley and season the soup with the salt.

9.33 Fruit juice

Stops diarrhea, promotes digestion, appetizing, harmonizes the stomach, relieves pain, detoxifying, reduces blood pressure, strengthens immune system, prevents cancer, reduces radiation damage.
Cooking time approx. 10 min
2 portions to 305g. / 176kcal. - (carb:93% / prot:7%)
100g.=57,54kcal. / protein 1,89g. fat:0,9g.
µg. - Ph:4,99 Na:2,24 Ka:37,45 Mg:2,36 Ca:6,04 Fe:0,21 Zn:0,05 Col.:0 Hsr.:4,3

Quantity of ingredients:
Orange 2 pieces / 150g. (yes)
Apple (sweet) 4 pieces / 300g. (yes)
Carrot 2 pieces / 150g. (yes)
Honey 1 table spoon / 10g. (yes)

Cooking instructions:
Peel oranges and carrots. Cut all ingredients into cubes so that they fit into the juicer and juice. Sweet with honey.

9.34 Hearty polenta mash

Strengths spleen and stomach, promotes watering, promotes digestion, detoxifying, promotes perspiration, reduces blood lipids, stimulates, dissolves stagnation, stimulates appetite, dissolves stagnation.
Cooking time approx. 10 min
2 portions to 207,5g. / 262kcal. - (carb:80% / prot:20%)
100g.=126,27kcal. / protein 5,65g. fat:5,94g.
µg. - Ph:6,71 Na:0,73 Ka:11,2 Mg:2,2 Ca:2,17 Fe:0,09 Zn:0,05 Col.:0 Hsr.:2,46

Quantity of ingredients:
Corn Grease (Polenta) 1 cup / 120g. (yes)
Onion (spring onion) 2 pieces / 40g. (yes)
Ginger fresh 1/2 teaspoon / 2g. (yes)
Nutmeg 1 pinch / 1g. (yes)
Salt 1 pinch / 1g. (little)

Olive oil 1 table spoon / 10g. (yes)
Turmeric (yellow root) 1 pinch / 1g. (yes)
Water 1 1/2 cups / 240g. (yes)

Cooking instructions:
Stir in the polenta in boiling water and let it swell for 7 min. Add green onion, grated ginger, turmeric, nutmeg, salt and olive oil and wait for 3 more minutes.

9.35 Kohlrabi in chervil sauce with potatoes

Reduces inflammation, lowers cholesterol, diuretic, conducts bowel winds, strengthens immune system, prevents cancer, promotes weight loss. Good to fight loss of appetite, flatulence, high blood pressure, depressions, diabetes, diarrhea.
Cooking time approx. 1 hour
Allergens: GL
4 portions to 316,75g. / 188kcal. - (carb:79% / prot:21%)
100g.=59,19kcal. / protein 8,66g. fat:2,51g.
µg. - Ph:2,95 Na:1,03 Ka:25,06 Mg:3,48 Ca:15,16 Fe:0,04 Zn:0,02 Col.:0,06 Hsr.:0,91

Quantity of ingredients:
Potato 6 pieces / 450g. (rec.)
Basic recipe for a vegetable soup (nutritious) 1 cup / 300g. (yes)
Potato 1/4 lbs - 4oz / 100g. (rec.)
Nutmeg 1 pinch / 0,2g. (yes)
Lemon peel 1/2 teaspoon / 2g. (yes)
Ginger fresh 1/2 teaspoon / 2g. (yes)
Lovage 1/2 teaspoon / 2g. (yes)
Kohlrabi 3/4 lbs / 300g. (yes)
Salt 1 pinch / 1g. (little)
Pepper (ground) 1 pinch / 0,2g. ()
Sour cream 15% fat 3 table spoons / 30g. (little)
Chervil dried 1 Bunch / 80g. (yes)

Cooking instructions:
Boil the potatoes in salted water.
Bring half of the vegetable stock to boil. Add the diced potatoes, nutmeg, lemon zest, ginger and lovage. Cover the potatoes and cook for about 10 minutes until soft and puree them with a blender until they are smooth.
Bring remaining vegetable stock to boil. Cut kohlrabi into cubes and add, cover and cook for about 8 minutes. Stir in the potato sauce and heat everything briefly.

Puree with the mixing stick chervil and sour cream. Mix the chervil cream with the kohlrabi vegetables.
Serve with the cooked, peeled potatoes.

9.36 Leek and potato gratin

Reduces inflammation, improves digestion, regenerates skin, supports urination, lowers cholesterol, promotes sweating, dissolves stagnation.
Cooking time approx. 1 hour
Allergens: CGL
4 portions to 346,5g. / 368kcal. - (carb:56% / prot:44%)
100g.=106,35kcal. / protein 7,73g. fat:16,47g.
µg. - Ph:3,43 Na:5,61 Ka:14,59 Mg:1,08 Ca:3,84 Fe:0,04 Zn:0,03 Col.:1,24 Hsr.:1,42

Quantity of ingredients:
Potato 1,1 lbs / 500g. (rec.)
Leek 1,1 lbs / 500g. (yes)
Apple (sour) 1 piece / 200g. (yes)
Crème fraiche cheese 1/4 lbs - 4oz / 125g. (little)
Basic recipe for a vegetable soup (nutritious) 1/4 cup / 20g. (yes)
Chicken yolk 1 piece / 20g. (little)
Emmental cheese 2 table spoons / 20g. (little)
Salt 1 pinch / 1g. (little)
Pepper (ground) 1 pinch / 0,5g. ()

Cooking instructions:
Wash the potatoes, peel, cut into very thin slices and pat dry. Place half in a flat greased baking dish.
Clean and wash leeks and cut into fine rings. Wash apple, peel and cut into thin slices. Spread the leek rings and apple slices on top. Put the remaining potato slices on top.
Mix crème fraîche, egg yolk, grated Emmentaler, salt and pepper, if necessary add some vegetable stock and pour over the casserole.
Bake at 200°C/392°F in the oven for about 45 to 50 minutes until golden brown. Cover with parchment paper after 30 minutes to prevent the burr from drying out.

9.37 Lettuce with fresh cheese

The bitter substances have diuretic effect and promote the blood circulation in the digestive area. Mustard improves thyroid function, relieves rheumatism symptoms.
Cooking time approx. 5 min
Allergens: AFM

1 portion to 260g. / 498kcal. - (carb:21% / prot:79%)
100g.=191,54kcal. / protein 22,11g. fat:52,97g.
µg. - Ph:138,82 Na:313,1 Ka:257,72 Mg:28,88 Ca:84,62 Fe:0,54 Zn:0,48 Col.:0,06
Hsr.:14,65

Quantity of ingredients:
Leaf salads (bitter) 2 portions / 60g. (yes)
Fresh cheese from soya 3/8 lbs - 6oz / 150g. (little)
Mustard 1 knife tip / 1g. (yes)
Lemon juice 1 dash / 3g. (yes)
Salt 1 pinch / 1g. (little)
Pepper (ground) 1 pinch / 0,5g. ()
Herbs various 2 teaspoons / 4g. (yes)
Black caraway 1 pinch / 1g. (yes)
Whole grain bread 2 slices / 40g. (yes)

Cooking instructions:
Wash lettuce and finely pluck.
Mix 150 ml cream cheese, splashes of mustard, splashes of lemon juice, 1 clove of garlic, chopped fresh herbs, pinch of pepper and crushed black cumin and pour over. Serve with wholemeal bread.

9.38 Mango banana yoghurt drink ice cold

Good to fight loss of appetite, oral mucosa inflammation. Regulates gastrointestinal function, chronic constipation. Prevents cancer. Diuretic, forcing spleen.
Cooking time approx. 5 min
Allergens: G
2 portions to 226g. / 121kcal. - (carb:87% / prot:13%)
100g.=53,54kcal. / protein 2,72g. fat:1,05g.
µg. - Ph:7,97 Na:3,73 Ka:51,04 Mg:5,37 Ca:11,04 Fe:0,07 Zn:0,04 Col.:0,28 Hsr.:2,87

Quantity of ingredients:
Mango juice 1/2 cup / 100g. (yes)
Yogurt (natural, 1.5% fat) 1/4 lbs - 4oz / 100g. (yes)
Mineral water 1/2 cup / 100g. (little)
Banana 1/2 piece / 150g. (yes)
Acerola fruit nectar or powder 1 teaspoon / 2g. (yes)

Cooking instructions:
Mix all the ingredients and 2-3 ice cubes in a blender.

9.39 Mashed banana

Eat 2 times a day, regulates gastrointestinal function
Cooking time approx. 7 min
1 portion to 150g. / 144kcal. - (carb:95% / prot:5%)
100g.=96kcal. / protein 1,65g. fat:0,3g.
µg. - Ph:28 Na:1 Ka:393 Mg:36 Ca:9 Fe:0,6 Zn:0,2 Col.:0 Hsr.:25

Quantity of ingredients:
Banana 1 piece / 150g. (yes)

Cooking instructions:
Mix the banana with the fork or purée with a blender. Leave to brown for at least 5 minutes.

9.40 Melanzani with olive oil and turmeric

Improves blood circulation, reduces inflammation, relieves pain, promotes digestion, helps to digest fat, supports urination, reduces blood pressure.
Cooking time approx. 30 min
Allergens: A
2 portions to 321,5g. / 432kcal. - (carb:47% / prot:53%)
100g.=134,37kcal. / protein 6,13g. fat:30,66g.
µg. - Ph:6,14 Na:10,38 Ka:42,8 Mg:2,74 Ca:3,55 Fe:0,09 Zn:0,05 Col.:0,02 Hsr.:4,84

Quantity of ingredients:
Aubergine 2 pieces / 300g. (yes)
Olive oil 4 table spoons / 60g. (yes)
Tomato 4 pieces / 200g. (yes)
Turmeric (yellow root) 1/2 teaspoon / 1g. (yes)
Ground 1 pinch / 1g. (yes)
Salt 1 pinch / 1g. (little)
White bread (wheat bread) 4 slices / 80g. (yes)

Cooking instructions:
Cut the Melanzani into slices and spread them with the tomatoes on a baking tray. Sprinkle with olive oil and then with turmeric, caraway and salt. Bake them in the tube 20 min.
Serve with the white bread.

9.41 Millet with pears

Refreshing and nourishing, promotes digestion, supports urination, good to fight cough, promotes perspiration, reduces blood lipids,

stimulates, dissolves stagnation, forces liver, strengthens the muscles, lowers cholesterol, antiparasitic.
Cooking time approx. 35 min
Allergens: G
5 portions to 238,4g. / 213kcal. - (carb:86% / prot:14%)
100g.=89,43kcal. / protein 3,91g. fat:3,24g.
µg. - Ph:1,89 Na:0,11 Ka:4,29 Mg:0,99 Ca:0,53 Fe:0,05 Zn:0,02 Col.:0 Hsr.:0,77

Quantity of ingredients:
Millet 1 cup / 120g. (yes)
Water 1 1/2 cups / 200g. (yes)
Grape juice red 1 1/2 cups / 240g. (yes)
Pear 4 pieces / 600g. (yes)
Ginger fresh 1/2 teaspoon / 2g. (yes)
Salt 1 pinch / 1g. (little)
Acerola fruit nectar or powder 1 teaspoon / 2g. (yes)
Cocoa 1 pinch / 1g. (yes)
Sunflower seeds 2 table spoons / 4g. (yes)
Barley malt 1/2 teaspoon / 2g. (yes)
Cream, sweet 30% 2 teaspoons / 20g. (little)

Cooking instructions:
Simmer the millet for 5 min and let it swell for another 30 min.

Then: In a hot pot, heat some grape juice; add chopped pears, very little grated ginger, a pinch of salt, acerola, a pinch of cocoa and sauté briefly; add the boiled millet, sunflower seeds, some barley malt to taste, 1 tsp cream per serving or a little butter.

9.42 Millet with shiitake mushrooms and avocado

Anti-inflammatory, good to fight swelling and pain, promotes spleen and kidney, diuretic, stimulates digestion, building up, eye-enhancing, detoxifying, nerve-strengthening, building up.
Cooking time approx. 20 min
Allergens: G
2 portions to 302g. / 560kcal. - (carb:57% / prot:43%)
100g.=185,26kcal. / protein 10,73g. fat:32,34g.
µg. - Ph:21,26 Na:1,29 Ka:57,67 Mg:12,21 Ca:3,72 Fe:0,53 Zn:0,22 Col.:1,49 Hsr.:14,77

Quantity of ingredients:
Millet 1 cup / 120g. (yes)
Shiitake, dried 1 oz / 25g. (yes)
Water 1 1/2 cups / 200g. (yes)

Ginger fresh 1/2 teaspoon / 2g. (yes)
Pepper (ground) 1 pinch / 0,5g. ()
Salt 1 pinch / 1g. (little)
Parsley 1 table spoon / 7g. (yes)
Peppers powder 1 pinch / 1g. (yes)
Butter organic 1 table spoon / 15g. (little)
Avocado 1 piece / 200g. (yes)
Lemon juice 1 dash / 3g. (yes)
Rucola 2 handful / 30g. ()

Cooking instructions:
In a saucepan with hot water, sprinkle the millet, add in strips cut shiitake mushrooms and some ginger and simmer; add a pinch of ground pepper, a little salt, plenty of parsley, a pinch of rose pepper, stir in a piece of butter.
In the meantime: place ½ peeled avocado per serving on one half of the plate: sprinkle with a little ground pepper, a small pinch of salt; drizzle with lemon juice; sprinkle a little chopped rocket or rose paprika over it. Put the millet dish on the other half of the plate.

9.43 Oat Congee

Strengthens immune system.
Cooking time approx. 2-4 hours
Allergens: A
3 portions to 275g. / 162kcal. - (carb:74% / prot:26%)
100g.=58,91kcal. / protein 7,04g. fat:2,87g.
µg. - Ph:5,76 Na:0,23 Ka:5,98 Mg:2,27 Ca:1,82 Fe:0,1 Zn:0,08 Col.:0 Hsr.:2,51

Quantity of ingredients:
Oat 1 cup / 125g. (yes)
Water 6 cups / 700g. (yes)

Cooking instructions:
Cook oats and water in a ratio of about 1: 6. The amount of water determines the thickness of the mash (pure matter of taste). The oats swell, so do not take much. Put the oats in a saucepan with good insulation and a heavy lid. It is important to simmer the oats after a short boil on the slightest flame, otherwise it burns. Cook the oat for 2-4 hours. The longer it cooks, the more he strengthens.

9.44 Oat flakes with aromatic spices

Stops diarrhea, promotes digestion, appetizing, harmonizes the stomach, relieves diarrhea, strengthens immune system, detoxifying and stimulating the immune system.

Cooking time approx. 25 min

Allergens: AH

3 portions to 208g. / 280kcal. - (carb:69% / prot:31%)
100g.=134,78kcal. / protein 6,73g. fat:10,72g.
µg. - Ph:11,3 Na:0,78 Ka:17,25 Mg:4,26 Ca:2,68 Fe:0,15 Zn:0,11 Col.:0 Hsr.:4,12

Quantity of ingredients:
Oat flakes (whole grain) 1 cup / 125g. (yes)
Walnuts 1 table spoon / 15g. (yes)
Hazelnuts 1 table spoon / 15g. (yes)
Water 1 1/2 cups / 240g. (yes)
Wakame 1 inch / 2g. (yes)
Apple (sweet) 1 piece / 220g. (yes)
Cardamom 3-4 capsules / 2g. (yes)
Lemon Balm (fresh) 3-4 leaves / 3g. (yes)
Acerola fruit nectar or powder 1 teaspoon / 2g. (yes)

Cooking instructions:
Roast oatmeal and nuts. Add hot water. Add cardamom, wakame and cook for 20 min. Add grated apple, acerola and lemon herb.

9.45 Oatmeal soup with spring onion and carrots

Reduces blood pressure, strengthens immune system, prevents cancer, reduces radiation damage, stimulates digestion, reduces pain, stimulates appetite, dissolves stagnation.

Cooking time approx. 30 min

Allergens: AG

3 portions to 266,33g. / 135kcal. - (carb:65% / prot:35%)
100g.=50,56kcal. / protein 3,87g. fat:5,59g.
µg. - Ph:3,67 Na:1,03 Ka:7,89 Mg:1,41 Ca:2,55 Fe:0,1 Zn:0,05 Col.:0,5 Hsr.:1,63

Quantity of ingredients:
Oat 6 table spoons / 48g. (yes)
Carrot 2 pieces / 200g. (yes)
Butter organic 1 table spoon / 15g. (little)
Nutmeg 1 pinch / 1g. (yes)
Lovage 1 stem / 15g. (yes)
Onion (spring onion) 2 pieces / 40g. (yes)
Water 2 cup / 480g. (yes)

Cooking instructions:

Roast the oats in butter, add salt and spices, pour in water and heat till it boils. After 10 min. add the grated carrots and lovage, cook for 10 minutes. Finely add chopped onion.

9.46 Paprika-tomato rice

Good to fight little cholesterol, diabetes. Low in protein, low fat content, little protein. Forcing spleen, dissolves stagnation, promotes weight loss. Good to fight immunodeficiency, loss of appetite, flatulence, high blood pressure, depressions.
Cooking time approx. 25 min
Allergens: L
3 portions to 324g. / 291kcal. - (carb:89% / prot:11%)
100g.=89,92kcal. / protein 7,63g. fat:2,54g.
µg. - Ph:10,3 Na:1,31 Ka:15,5 Mg:9,5 Ca:22,5 Fe:0,14 Zn:0,06 Col.:0 Hsr.:4,12

Quantity of ingredients:
Onion white 1 piece / 50g. (yes)
Peppers 4 pieces / 120g. (yes)
Bay leaf 2 pieces / 1g. (yes)
Clove 2 pieces / 1g. (yes)
Basic recipe for a vegetable soup (nutritious) 7/8 lbs / 400g. (yes)
Champignon 1/8 lbs - 2oz / 60g. (yes)
Parsley 1/2 oz / 20g. (yes)
Pepper (ground) 1 pinch / 0,2g. ()
Peppers (rose peppers) 1 pinch / 0,2g. (yes)
Tomato 1/4 lbs - 4oz / 120g. (yes)

Cooking instructions:
Finely chop the onion. Cut the peppers into fine strips.
Heat margarine in a saucepan, sauté onions and peppers, and rice.
Add the vegetable stock, add cloves and bay leaves and leave to simmer in a closed pot for approx. 20 minutes. Cut the tomato meat into 1 cm cubes and add to the rice 5 minutes before the end of cooking.

9.47 Pear juice

Promotes digestion, supports urination.
Cooking time approx. 5 min
2 portions to 300g. / 180kcal. - (carb:93% / prot:7%)
100g.=60kcal. / protein 1,8g. fat:1,2g.
µg. - Ph:7,5 Na:1 Ka:62,5 Mg:3,5 Ca:4,5 Fe:0,15 Zn:0,05 Col.:0 Hsr.:7,5

Quantity of ingredients:
Pear 3 pieces / 600g. (yes)

Cooking instructions:
Peel pears thinly (vitamins under the skin) and core. Juice in the juicer.

9.48 Polenta with peach

Relieves fatigue, forcing spleen, diuretic, strengthens the defense, good to fight fungi infections, lets urine and bile juice flow, prevents the aging process, strengthens brain cells.
Cooking time approx. 20 min
3 portions to 254g. / 197kcal. - (carb:89% / prot:11%)
100g.=77,56kcal. / protein 4,48g. fat:0,6g.
µg. - Ph:2,76 Na:0,12 Ka:11,83 Mg:0,93 Ca:1,02 Fe:0,05 Zn:0,02 Col.:0 Hsr.:1,56

Quantity of ingredients:
Water 1 1/2 cups / 240g. (yes)
Corn Grease (Polenta) 1 cup / 120g. (yes)
Peaches 2-3 pieces / 400g. (yes)
Vanilla pod 1 pinch / 1g. (yes)
Chili (pod or ground) 1 pinch / 0,1g. (yes)
Cinnamon ground 1 pinch / 1g. (yes)

Cooking instructions:
Pour the polenta into a pan of hot water with constant stirring until the polenta has the desired consistency. Pull the polenta from the fire and let it soak for 10 minutes.
Wash fresh peaches and cut into quarters. Pour into the finished polenta the peaches, add the vanilla and add Chili to taste, stir and let it go for 3 minutes.
Winter varieties: Pickled fruit, pear, apples.

9.49 Potato cream with herbs and fresh cheese

Good to fight loss of appetite, constipation, bloating and nausea.
Improves digestion, supports urination, prevents cancer, forcing spleen, dissolves stagnation, relaxing and reassuring.
Cooking time approx. 25 min
Allergens: G
2 portions to 218,5g. / 217kcal. - (carb:14% / prot:86%)
100g.=99,31kcal. / protein 8,76g. fat:11,22g.
µg. - Ph:18,66 Na:18,04 Ka:73,64 Mg:4,87 Ca:13,9 Fe:0,13 Zn:0,09 Col.:4,84 Hsr.:2,24

Quantity of ingredients:
Potato (mealy) 5/8 lbs - 8oz / 250g. (rec.)
Fresh cheese 3 oz / 80g. (little)

Yogurt (natural, 1.5% fat) 3 table spoons / 45g. (yes)
Chives 1/2 bunch / 50g. (yes)
Basil (fresh) 1 teaspoon / 4g. (yes)
Parsley 1 teaspoon / 4g. (yes)
Dill 1/2 teaspoon / 2g. (yes)
Salt 1 pinch / 1g. (little)
Black caraway 1 pinch / 0,5g. (yes)
Pepper (ground) 1 pinch / 0,5g. ()

Cooking instructions:
Softly steam the potatoes in the pan, peel them and press through the potato press.
Mix cream cheese, yoghurt and herbs under the potatoes, season with salt, crushed black cumin and pepper.

9.50 Potato gnocchi with vegetables and basil sauce

Strengthens immune system, promotes weight loss. Good to fight immunodeficiency, loss of appetite, flatulence, high blood pressure. Relaxing and reassuring.
Cooking time approx. 1 hour
Allergens: ACGL
4 portions to 290,25g. / 167kcal. - (carb:75% / prot:25%)
100g.=57,45kcal. / protein 6,54g. fat:4,63g.
µg. - Ph:3,26 Na:1,11 Ka:13,57 Mg:2,45 Ca:9,39 Fe:0,06 Zn:0,02 Col.:1,36 Hsr.:1,49

Quantity of ingredients:
Potato 5/8 lbs - 8oz / 250g. (rec.)
Wheat flour 1 oz / 25g. (yes)
Wheat semolina 1/2 oz / 15g. (yes)
Chicken yolk 1 piece / 20g. (little)
Nutmeg 1 pinch / 0,2g. (yes)
Basic recipe for a vegetable soup (nutritious) 1 cup / 250g. (yes)
Celery root 1/8 lbs - 2oz / 50g. (yes)
Lemon peel 1/2 teaspoon / 2g. (yes)
Ginger fresh 1/2 teaspoon / 2g. (yes)
Nutmeg 1 pinch / 0,2g. (yes)
Basil (fresh) 1 Bunch / 125g. (yes)
Crème fraiche cheese 1 table spoon / 20g. (little)
Salt 1 pinch / 1g. (little)
Pepper (ground) 1 pinch / 0,2g. ()
Carrot 1/4 lbs - 4oz / 100g. (yes)
Zucchini 1/4 lbs - 4oz / 100g. (yes)
Cauliflower 1/4 lbs - 4oz / 100g. (yes)

Broccoli 1/4 lbs - 4oz / 100g. (yes)
Salt 1 pinch / 1g. (little)

Cooking instructions:
Steam the potatoes gently, peel and pass hot through the potato press.
Process the hot potatoes with flour, semolina, egg, nutmeg and salt to a
smooth dough. Let dough rest for 3o minutes.
Make small rolls (2 cm) out of the dough with flour-dusted hands, cut off
1 cm thin slices. To create the typical gnocchi shape, gently dab the
dough pieces with your thumb. Leave the gnocchi in lightly boiling
salted water for 6 - 8 minutes. Lift the gnocchi out of the pot with the
skimmer.

Heat the vegetable stock till it boils. Add diced celery, grated lemon
peel, finely chopped ginger and 1 pinch of nutmeg. Cover and simmer
for about 10 minutes. Using the blender, puree the vegetable broth,
celery, chopped basil and créme fraiche into a smooth sauce. Season
with salt and nutmeg.

Cut carrots, zucchini, cauliflower and broccoli into small pieces and
cook covered in a sieve over steam for 8 minutes until firm.
Heat the sauce again and add to the vegetables and arrange over the
gnocchi.

9.51 Potato-basil soup

Reduces inflammation, improves digestion, supports urination, lowers
cholesterol, reduces blood pressure, strengthens immune system,
prevents cancer, reduces radiation damage, antioxidative, dissolves
stagnation.
Cooking time approx. 25 min
Allergens: L
4 portions to 330g. / 96kcal. - (carb:69% / prot:31%)
100g.=28,94kcal. / protein 3,23g. fat:2,99g.
µg. - Ph:1,91 Na:3,35 Ka:13,03 Mg:0,61 Ca:2,91 Fe:0,03 Zn:0,01 Col.:0 Hsr.:1,9

Quantity of ingredients:
Water 2 cups / 450g. (yes)
Potato 4 pieces / 200g. (rec.)
Carrot 2 pieces / 100g. (yes)
Celery root 1 piece / 500g. (yes)
Pepper (ground) 1 pinch / 0,5g. ()
Ground 1 pinch / 1g. (yes)
Garlic 1 clove / 3g. (yes)

Salt 1 pinch / 1g. (little)
Lemon 1 teaspoon / 3g. (yes)
Basil (fresh) 1 Bunch / 50g. (yes)
Peppers powder 1 pinch / 1g. (yes)
Sugar cane sugar 1 pinch / 1g. (yes)
Olive oil 1 table spoon / 10g. (yes)

Cooking instructions:
Peeled and chopped 4 medium potatoes in a pot of hot water and 2
chopped medium carrots, a piece of celery root, a pinch of pepper, a
pinch of ground cumin, crushed a small clove of garlic, a pinch of salt, 1
teaspoon of lemon juice, simmer until the Vegetables is soft.

Add 1 bunch finely chopped basil into one half of the soup and puree
everything; stir in the other half of the basil; with rose paprika, a pinch of
whole cane sugar, 1 tablespoon of olive oil or butter, freshly ground
pepper, salt to taste.

9.52 Pumpkin curry

Promotes digestion and sweating, Dissolves stagnation, strengthens
lungs and spleen, diuretic, reduces blood glucose,
forcing spleen and digestive system, detoxifying, strengthens the
muscles and bones.
Cooking time approx. 20 min
3 portions to 251g. / 193kcal. - (carb:63% / prot:37%)
100g.=77,03kcal. / protein 2,72g. fat:10,61g.
µg. - Ph:5,14 Na:0,86 Ka:16,34 Mg:2,68 Ca:2,29 Fe:0,06 Zn:0,02 Col.:0 Hsr.:1,54

Quantity of ingredients:
Pumpkin 3/4 lbs / 300g. (yes)
Olive oil 2 table spoons / 30g. (yes)
Coriander 1 pinch / 1g. (yes)
Pepper (ground) 1 pinch / 0,5g. ()
Curry 1 pinch / 1g. (yes)
Water 1/4 cup / 50g. (yes)
Salt 1 pinch / 1g. (little)
Parsley 1 table spoon / 7g. (yes)
Cardamom 1 pinch / 1g. (yes)
Turmeric (yellow root) 1 pinch / 1g. (yes)
Rice (whole grain) 1/2 cup / 60g. (yes)
Water 3 cups / 300g. (yes)
Salt 1 pinch / 1g. (little)

Cooking instructions:
Heat olive oil in pan. Steam the pumpkin cut in cubes, season with cilantro, pepper and curry, simmer with a little water, salt with sea salt, add chopped parsley with cardamom and turmeric, simmer on a small fire for about 10 minutes, depending on the pumpkin, the pumpkin should still be firm.

Place the rice in salted water, bring to the boil and let it simmer over low heat for about 15 minutes.

9.53 Pumpkin-yoghurt soup

Relaxes, reduces blood pressure, strengthens immune system, promotes weight loss. Good to fight immunodeficiency, loss of appetite, flatulence, depressions, diabetes, diarrhea.
Cooking time approx. 15 min
Allergens: GL
4 portions to 239g. / 68kcal. - (carb:83% / prot:17%)
100g.=28,45kcal. / protein 2,37g. fat:1,31g.
µg. - Ph:1,79 Na:0,9 Ka:6,6 Mg:2,8 Ca:10,96 Fe:0,02 Zn:0,01 Col.:0,05 Hsr.:0,35

Quantity of ingredients:
Basic recipe for a vegetable soup (nutritious) 1 cup / 300g. (yes)
Hokkaido pumpkin 1,1 lbs / 500g. (yes)
Ginger fresh 1/2 teaspoon / 2g. (yes)
Fennel seeds ground 1/2 teaspoon / 1g. (yes)
Anise (Common Fennel) 1/4 teaspoon / 1g. (yes)
Yogurt (natural, 1.5% fat) 3/8 lbs - 6oz / 150g. (yes)
Peppermint 2 leaves / 1g. (yes)
Salt 1 pinch / 1g. (little)

Cooking instructions:
Heat the vegetable broth (after the basic recipe) till it boils. Add diced pumpkin, chopped ginger, crushed fennel seeds and anise. Bring the soup to the boil and simmer for about 12 minutes until the pumpkin is soft.
Remove soup from the heat. Puree the soup with the yoghurt with the blender. Serve soup with finely chopped mint sprinkled.

9.54 Quick zucchini soup

Diuretic, supports urination. Strengthens gastrointestinal function, expands blood vessels, prevents cancer, prevents diseases (in the elderly). Stimulates liver function, detoxifying.

Cooking time approx. 10 min
4 portions to 241,5g. / 42kcal. - (carb:46% / prot:54%)
100g.=17,29kcal. / protein 1,76g. fat:2,04g.
µg. - Ph:3,81 Na:0,41 Ka:29,78 Mg:3,2 Ca:5,37 Fe:0,21 Zn:0,01 Col.:0 Hsr.:2,85

Quantity of ingredients:
Zucchini 2-3 pieces / 500g. (yes)
Onion white 1 piece / 50g. (yes)
Corn germ oil 2 table spoons / 6g. (yes)
Parsley 1 table spoon / 7g. (yes)
Chives 1 teaspoon / 3g. (yes)
Water 2 cup / 400g. (yes)

Cooking instructions:
Fry chopped onion in oil. Add sliced zucchini and sauté well. Pour with water. Chop parsley and chives, add and puree everything.

9.55 Raw celery salad

Refreshing, forcing spleen, provides Vitamin C, strengthens digestive system, detoxifying, improves blood circulation, strengthens liver and kidney, detoxifying, strengthens the muscles, promotes weight loss.
Cooking time approx. 15 min
Allergens: HLN
1 portion to 327g. / 590kcal. - (carb:26% / prot:74%)
100g.=180,43kcal. / protein 6,84g. fat:51,9g.
µg. - Ph:58,86 Na:64,97 Ka:271,14 Mg:26,75 Ca:65,8 Fe:0,65 Zn:0,25 Col.:0,12 Hsr.:40,4

Quantity of ingredients:
Celery root 1/4 piece / 125g. (yes)
Celery sticks 2 branches / 30g. (yes)
Sesame oil 4 table spoons / 40g. (yes)
Almond puree 2 table spoons / 20g. (yes)
Pepper (ground) 1 pinch / 0,5g. ()
Salt 1 pinch / 1g. (little)
Lemon 1/2 cup / 50g. (yes)
Orange juice 1/2 cup / 60g. (yes)
Peppers powder 1 pinch / 1g. (yes)

Cooking instructions:
Finely grate the celeriac; cut the celeriac into small pieces; celery leaves, cut into small pieces, blanch and combine everything.

Dressing: sesame oil, almond paste, pepper, salt, lemon and fresh orange juice, stir well some rose paprika; mix with the celery and let it pass through.

9.56 Refreshing cucumber soup with potatoes

Diuretic, detoxifying, suppresses conversion of sugar into fat, lowers cholesterol, prevents cancer, reduces inflammation, improves digestion, lowers cholesterol, dissolves stagnation, improves blood circulation, stimulates appetite.
Cooking time approx. 15 min
Allergens: GN
3 portions to 307,33g. / 148kcal. - (carb:70% / prot:30%)
100g.=48,26kcal. / protein 3,93g. fat:5,09g.
µg. - Ph:3,72 Na:0,77 Ka:23,54 Mg:1,43 Ca:2 Fe:0,05 Zn:0,02 Col.:0 Hsr.:1,19

Quantity of ingredients:
Sesame oil 1 table spoon / 10g. (yes)
Potato 4 pieces / 300g. (rec.)
Onion (spring onion) 3 pieces / 60g. (yes)
Pepper (ground) 1 pinch / 0,5g. ()
Nutmeg 1 pinch / 1g. (yes)
Salt 1 pinch / 1g. (little)
Lemon 1/2 piece / 25g. (yes)
Cucumber 2 pieces / 500g. (yes)
Cream, sweet 30% 1 table spoon / 10g. (little)
Dill 1 table spoon / 15g. (yes)

Cooking instructions:
Sauté sesame oil, chopped potatoes, plenty of spring onions in a hot pot; add pepper, a little nutmeg, salt, lemon juice, hot water, diced cucumber; simmer for about 10 minutes and then puree; add some sweet cream as you like, and fresh dill.

Variation: Add a little chili, oregano, thyme or rosemary to soften the cooling effect.

9.57 Rhubarb and apple jelly

Antioxidants, lots of vitamin C, laxative, relieves pain, detoxifying, warms stomach and spleen, improves blood circulation.
Cooking time approx. 15 min
2 portions to 276,5g. / 180kcal. - (carb:96% / prot:4%)
100g.=65,1kcal. / protein 1,19g. fat:0,58g.
µg. - Ph:14,75 Na:1,5 Ka:93,5 Mg:7,42 Ca:12,73 Fe:0,29 Zn:0,07 Col.:0 Hsr.:6,21

Quantity of ingredients:
Apple juice (natural cloudy) 1 cup / 300g. (yes)
Corn starch 1 oz / 30g. (yes)
Honey 1/2 oz / 20g. (yes)
Vanilla sugar natural 1 pinch / 0,5g. (yes)
Cinnamon ground 1 pinch / 0,5g. (yes)
Peppermint 2 leaves / 2g. (yes)

Cooking instructions:
Add the cornstarch to a 1/2 cup apple juice.
Simmer the rhubarb in 1 cup of water for 10 min.
Add the remaining apple juice and the cornstarch, stir, heat till it boils again.
Sweet with honey and season with vanilla and cinnamon. Spread the mixture on dessert bowls and garnish with mint.

9.58 Rice congee with honey pear and black sesame

Promotes digestion, supports urination, good to fight blood circulation disorders, thromboses, risk of embolism, high blood pressure, a headache, heart attack and stroke.
Cooking time approx. 10 min - 3 hours
Allergens: N
2 portions to 271,5g. / 158kcal. - (carb:0% / prot:0%)
100g.=58,38kcal. / protein 2,43g. fat:1,55g.
µg. - Ph:9,61 Na:0,87 Ka:36,87 Mg:70,29 Ca:68,61 Fe:0,18 Zn:0,12 Col.:0 Hsr.:5,76

Quantity of ingredients:
Basic recipe for a rice soup (Congee) 1 1/2 cups / 240g. (yes)
Pear 2 pieces / 300g. (yes)
Sesame, black 1 teaspoon / 3g. (yes)

Cooking instructions:
Cook rice congee according to basic recipe.
Fill pot with 3 cm of water and heat till it boils. Quarter the pears (with the skin and seeds) and simmer them covered with black sesame for 10 minutes. Mix with the rice.

9.59 Rice with parsnips

Rich in vitamins, minerals potassium and zinc. Good to fight blood circulation disorders, thrombose, risk of embolism, high blood pressure, a headache, heart attack and stroke, yeast infections.

Cooking time approx. 45 min
3 portions to 261,33g. / 206kcal. - (carb:78% / prot:22%)
100g.=78,95kcal. / protein 5,16g. fat:4,52g.
µg. - Ph:6,72 Na:0,7 Ka:31,66 Mg:2,54 Ca:3,53 Fe:0,05 Zn:0,07 Col.:0 Hsr.:4,06

Quantity of ingredients:
Rice variety any 1 cup / 120g. (yes)
Water 1 1/2 cups / 200g. (yes)
Salt 1 pinch / 1g. (little)
Parsnip 3-4 pieces / 450g. (yes)
Olive oil 1 table spoon / 10g. (yes)
Sage 1 teaspoon / 3g. (yes)

Cooking instructions:
Peel the parsnips and cut into slices. Fry for a short time in oil. Add the rice and fry again for a short time. Add the water and cook it at least 30 min. Sprinkle with fresh chopped sage.

9.60 Rice with stewed vegetables

Reduces blood pressure, strengthens immune system, prevents cancer, reduces radiation damage, extremely low fat content, good to fight blood circulation disorders, thrombose, risk of embolism, a headache, heart attack and stroke. Is diuretic.
Cooking time approx. 20 min
Allergens: L
2 portions to 310,5g. / 166kcal. - (carb:82% / prot:18%)
100g.=53,62kcal. / protein 4,33g. fat:2,25g.
µg. - Ph:8,31 Na:2,83 Ka:26,32 Mg:3,14 Ca:5,9 Fe:0,2 Zn:0,07 Col.:0 Hsr.:6,32

Quantity of ingredients:
Rice variety any 1/2 cup / 60g. (yes)
Water 3 cups / 300g. (yes)
Lemon peel 1 piece / 3g. (yes)
Water 1/2 cup / 0g. (yes)
Carrot 2 pieces / 180g. (yes)
Celery sticks 1/2 piece / 5g. (yes)
Champignon 1/2 cup / 50g. (yes)
Cress 2 table spoons / 20g. (yes)
Linseed oil 1 dash / 3g. (yes)

Cooking instructions:
Cook rice according to basic recipe with a piece of lemon peel.
Steam chopped carrots, celery and mushrooms until soft.

Then sprinkle with cress. Then add a dash of high quality cold oil.

9.61 Roasted barley patties

Improves digestion, lowers cholesterol, good to fight diarrhea, ulceration, joint pain, stomach problems. Promotes spleen and liver, reduces blood pressure, strengthens immune system, prevents cancer, reduces radiation damage, stimulates liver function.
Cooking time approx. 1 1/2 hours
Allergens: ACN
3 portions to 292,67g. / 398kcal. - (carb:63% / prot:37%)
100g.=135,99kcal. / protein 8,38g. fat:19,69g.
µg. - Ph:7,07 Na:4,18 Ka:17,24 Mg:2,02 Ca:2,5 Fe:0,08 Zn:0,04 Col.:2,76 Hsr.:2,93

Quantity of ingredients:
Water 1 1/2 cups / 250g. (yes)
Barley grouts 1 cup / 120g. (yes)
Potato 1 piece / 140g. (rec.)
Carrot 1 piece / 120g. (yes)
Champignon 2-3 pieces / 25g. (yes)
Chicken egg 1 piece / 55g. (little)
Onion white 1 piece / 50g. (yes)
Ginger fresh 1/2 teaspoon / 1g. (yes)
Pepper (ground) 1 pinch / 0,5g. ()
Salt 1 pinch / 1g. (little)
Lemon 1/2 piece / 15g. (yes)
Parsley 2 table spoons / 15g. (yes)
Peppers powder 1 pinch / 1g. (yes)
Sesame oil 2 table spoons / 50g. (yes)
Bread roll 1 piece / 35g. (yes)

Cooking instructions:
Preparation:
Place 2 large cups of hot water in a saucepan; add 1 large cup of barley porridge; simmer for 2 minutes while stirring; then let it swell for 20 minutes on the switched off stove; take down and let cool.
Cook in boiling water 1 large potato, chopped and cut.
Soak 1 roll in hot water and squeeze well.
Then: Mix the barley groats and crushed the potato. Add 1 grated carrot, 2 - 3 chopped mushrooms, 1 egg, 1 finely chopped onion, 1/2 teaspoon grated ginger, a pinch of pepper, a pinch of salt, a little lemon juice, chopped parsley, plenty of rose paprika; knead well and form patties; heat sesame oil in a hot pan; fry the patties for about 15 minutes over a gentle heat; turn at half time.

Also fits well: lettuce, soybean vegetables.

9.62 Roasted millet with Celery sticks

Promotes spleen and kidney, diuretic, promoting metabolism.
Cooking time approx. 30 min
Allergens: L
2 portions to 228g. / 400kcal. - (carb:82% / prot:18%)
100g.=175,44kcal. / protein 7g. fat:2,58g.
µg. - Ph:22,21 Na:4,29 Ka:15,63 Mg:11,94 Ca:5,5 Fe:0,62 Zn:0,24 Col.:0 Hsr.:6,31

Quantity of ingredients:
Millet 1 cup / 120g. (yes)
Water 1 1/2 cups / 240g. (yes)
Celery sticks 2 rods / 50g. (yes)
Herbs various 1 table spoon / 10g. (yes)
Water 2 table spoons / 30g. (yes)
Salt 1 pinch / 1g. (little)
Sage 3-4 leaves / 2g. (yes)
Cress 1 teaspoon / 3g. (yes)

Cooking instructions:
Roast millet briefly, pour over water, heat till it boils and let stand for 20 min. to swell.

Cut celery into small pieces and mix with water, salt and fresh herbs and cook for 10 min. Add to the millet. Sprinkle fresh sage or watercress over it.

9.63 Roasted millet with plum compote

Supports urination, promotes spleen and kidney, strengthens the defense. Good to fight fungi infections.
Cooking time approx. 30 min
4 portions to 218,25g. / 139kcal. - (carb:85% / prot:15%)
100g.=63,8kcal. / protein 3,57g. fat:1,24g.
µg. - Ph:2,99 Na:0,1 Ka:4,37 Mg:1,68 Ca:0,78 Fe:0,09 Zn:0,03 Col.:0 Hsr.:0,93

Quantity of ingredients:
Millet 1 cup / 120g. (yes)
Water 1 1/2 cups / 250g. (yes)
Plum 1 1/2 cups / 250g. (yes)
Vanilla pod 1 pinch / 1g. (yes)
Water 5/8 lbs - 8oz / 250g. (yes)

Cinnamon ground 1 pinch / 1g. (yes)
Acerola fruit nectar or powder 1/2 teaspoon / 1g. (yes)

Cooking instructions:
Roast millet briefly, pour over water, heat till it boils and let stand for 20 min. to swell.

Cook plums with water, vanilla and cinnamon 10 min. then strain. Add acerola and add to the millet.

9.64 Rosemary Potatoes

Reduces Inflammation, improves digestion, regenerates skin, supports urination, lowers cholesterol. Rosemary stimulates digestion, strengthens lung, promotes spleen and kidney, dries out.
Cooking time approx. 30 min
2 portions to 216,5g. / 188kcal. - (carb:76% / prot:24%)
100g.=87,07kcal. / protein 4,21g. fat:5,25g.
µg. - Ph:11,51 Na:0,72 Ka:82,88 Mg:4,72 Ca:1,86 Fe:0,1 Zn:0,07 Col.:0 Hsr.:3,64

Quantity of ingredients:
Potato 6-8 pieces / 420g. (rec.)
Salt (herbal) 1 pinch / 1g. (little)
Olive oil 1 table spoon / 10g. (yes)
Rosemary 1 teaspoon / 2g. (yes)

Cooking instructions:
Cut the potatoes into half´s, apply a little olive oil on the cut surface, then salt, sprinkle 2 - 3 rosemary needles on the potatoes.
Place the potatoes on the baking tray and bake them in the preheated oven for approx. 25 minutes to 190°C/374°F.

9.65 Semolina porridge with banana

Regulates gastrointestinal function, reduces inflammation, antiallergic, good to fight blood circulation disorders.
Cooking time approx. 15 min
Allergens: AG
1 portion to 284g. / 307kcal. - (carb:66% / prot:34%)
100g.=108,1kcal. / protein 10,57g. fat:10,72g.
µg. - Ph:116,7 Na:93,56 Ka:218,89 Mg:28,56 Ca:92,08 Fe:0,64 Zn:0,36 Col.:7,61
Hsr.:12,85

Quantity of ingredients:
Cow's milk (whole milk 3.5% fat) 3/4 cup - 6 oz / 200g. (yes)

Spelled semolina 3 table spoons / 30g. (yes)
Butter organic 1 teaspoon / 4g. (little)
Banana 1/2 piece / 50g. (yes)

Cooking instructions:
Heat the half of the milk in a small pot. Add the semolina and boil it
shortly in the milk. Let it swell at low heat for 3 minutes with constant
stirring. Remove the pot from the heat, add the remaining milk with the
snow bean and place the mush in a small bowl. Add the butter and the
battered banana.
For adults, a pinch of cinnamon can be spread over it.

9.66 Semolina soup with vegetables

Reduces blood pressure, strengthens immune system, prevents cancer,
forcing spleen, dissolves stagnation, promotes weight loss. Good to
fight immunodeficiency, loss of appetite, flatulence, high blood
pressure, depressions, diabetes, diarrhea, rheumatism, heartburn,
twelffinger intestinal ulcers.
Cooking time approx. 20 min
Allergens: AGL
3 portions to 237,67g. / 105kcal. - (carb:85% / prot:15%)
100g.=44,32kcal. / protein 2,38g. fat:4,24g.
µg. - Ph:2,88 Na:3,04 Ka:8,54 Mg:9,5 Ca:37,49 Fe:0,11 Zn:0,03 Col.:0 Hsr.:1,7

Quantity of ingredients:
Basic recipe for a vegetable soup (nutritious) 2 cup / 500g. (yes)
Wheat semolina 2 table spoons / 20g. (yes)
Lovage 1/2 teaspoon / 2g. (yes)
Basil (fresh) 1/2 teaspoon / 1g. (yes)
Nutmeg 1 pinch / 0,1g. (yes)
Carrot 1/4 lbs - 4oz / 100g. (yes)
Celery root 1/8 lbs - 2oz / 50g. (yes)
Cream, sweet 30% 3 table spoons / 30g. (little)
Parsley 1 table spoon / 10g. (yes)

Cooking instructions:
Roast wheat grits without fat in a pan. Roast the chopped carrots and
celery briefly. Add the vegetable soup (Basic recipe for a vegetable
soup). Season with lovage, nutmeg and let it 10 min. simmer.
Stir in the cream before serving and garnish with parsley.

9.67 Strawberry yoghurt and almond puree mix

Relieves pain and inflammation in rheumatism. Good to fight acute or chronic constipation of the intestine. Little laxative. Relieves pain, detoxifying, bactericide.
Cooking time approx. 5 min
Allergens: GH
3 portions to 303,67g. / 134kcal. - (carb:73% / prot:27%)
100g.=44,13kcal. / protein 4,53g. fat:3,36g.
µg. - Ph:4,67 Na:1,48 Ka:16,91 Mg:1,74 Ca:5,71 Fe:0,09 Zn:0,02 Col.:0,12 Hsr.:2,16

Quantity of ingredients:
Strawberries 1,5 lbs / 700g. (yes)
Honey 1 teaspoon / 3g. (yes)
Acerola fruit nectar or powder 1 teaspoon / 2g. (yes)
Almond puree 2 teaspoons / 6g. (yes)

Cooking instructions:
Puree yoghurt, strawberries, acerola, honey and almond paste in a blender.

9.68 Tea Black tea (Russian tea)

Black tea improves blood circulation.
Cooking time approx. 10 min
1 portion to 125g. / 7kcal. - (carb:3% / prot:97%)
100g.=5,6kcal. / protein 1,28g. fat:0,26g.
µg. - Ph:11,92 Na:1,2 Ka:72,32 Mg:7,96 Ca:16,52 Fe:0,07 Zn:0,1 Col.:0 Hsr.:13,12

Quantity of ingredients:
Black tea 1 table spoon / 5g. (yes)
Water 1 cup / 120g. (yes)

Cooking instructions:
For each cup you use a teaspoonful or a teabag.
Pour green tea only with 60 to 80 ° C / 140 to 176 °F hot water, otherwise it will be bitter.
If the tea has a stimulating effect, let it draw for two to three minutes. It has a calming effect for a duration of five minutes (no longer, otherwise it will be bitter!).
Another method: Pour the tea leaves with about 70 ° C / 158 °F hot water and pour the water immediately again. Then just pour hot water again. The bitter substances disappear, and the tea gets a milder aroma.

9.69 Tea from chamomile

Good to fight flatulence, nausea, intestinal cramps, diarrhea, inflammation of the oral mucosa, influenza infections, stomach and intestinal mucosa infections, badly healing wounds, nausea, colds, skin rashes, inflammation in the genital and anal area.
Cooking time approx. 10 min
1 portion to 123g. / 0kcal. - (carb:0% / prot:0%)
100g.=0kcal. / protein 0g. fat:0g.
µg. - Ph:0 Na:0,98 Ka:0 Mg:0,98 Ca:4,88 Fe:0,01 Zn:0,1 Col.:0 Hsr.:0

Quantity of ingredients:
Chamomile 1 teaspoon / 3g. (yes)
Water 1 cup / 120g. (yes)

Cooking instructions:
Heat the water till it boils and put it aside. Chamomile flowers added and 10 min. to let go.

9.70 Tea from coriander

Coriander promotes digestion, diaphoretic.
Cooking time approx. 10 min
4 portions to 125,75g. / 2kcal. - (carb:100% / prot:0%)
100g.=1,79kcal. / protein 0g. fat:0g.
µg. - Ph:0,15 Na:0,07 Ka:0,44 Mg:0,18 Ca:0,57 Fe:0 Zn:0,01 Col.:0 Hsr.:0

Quantity of ingredients:
Coriander 1 teaspoon / 3g. (yes)
Water 2 cup / 500g. (yes)

Cooking instructions:
Heat the water till it boils and put it aside. Add coriander and 10 min. to let go. Sweet to taste with honey. Strain when pouring.

9.71 Tea from fennel

Harmonizes stomach, less bloating.
Cooking time approx. 10 min
4 portions to 130g. / 0kcal. - (carb:0% / prot:0%)
100g.=0kcal. / protein 0g. fat:0g.
µg. - Ph:0 Na:0,06 Ka:0 Mg:0,06 Ca:0,3 Fe:0 Zn:0,01 Col.:0 Hsr.:0

Quantity of ingredients:
Fennel tea 2 table spoons / 20g. (yes)
Water 2 cup / 500g. (yes)

Cooking instructions:
Heat the water till it boils and put it aside. Add fennel tea and 10 min. to let go. Sweet to taste with honey. Strain when pouring.

9.72 Tea from peppermint with white sugar

Peppermint relaxes, frees lungs and nose (inhaling), regulates cycle, detoxifying.
Cooking time approx. 15 min
2 portions to 255g. / 8kcal. - (carb:91% / prot:9%)
100g.=2,94kcal. / protein 0,13g. fat:0,02g.
µg. - Ph:0,24 Na:0,3 Ka:0,92 Mg:0,35 Ca:1,97 Fe:0,01 Zn:0,02 Col.:0 Hsr.:0

Quantity of ingredients:
Peppermint 1 table spoon / 7g. (yes)
Water 2 cup / 500g. (yes)
Sugar candy white 1 teaspoon / 3g. (yes)

Cooking instructions:
Heat the water till it boils and put it aside. Add peppermint and 10 min. to let go. Strain. Sweet to taste with honey.

9.73 Tea from valerian

Lowers blood pressure, cramp-dissolving, relief of climacteric symptoms, against depressions.
Cooking time approx. 10 min
1 portion to 127g. / 0kcal. - (carb:0% / prot:0%)
100g.=0kcal. / protein 0g. fat:0g.
µg. - Ph:0 Na:0,98 Ka:0 Mg:0,98 Ca:4,92 Fe:0,01 Zn:0,09 Col.:0 Hsr.:0

Quantity of ingredients:
Valerian 1 teaspoon / 2g. (yes)
Water 1 cup / 125g. (yes)

Cooking instructions:
Brew dried valerian tea with boiling water and cover for about 10 minutes. Strain the tea and drink warm.

9.74 Tea Green tea

Green tea promotes digestion, supports urination, dissolves mucus, detoxifying, stimulates nerves, reduces blood lipids, lowers cholesterol, reduces inflammation.

Cooking time approx. 10 min
1 portion to 122g. / 2kcal. - (carb:20% / prot:80%)
100g.=1,64kcal. / protein 0g. fat:0g.
µg. - Ph:5,61 Na:1,07 Ka:27,59 Mg:4,07 Ca:9,43 Fe:0,03 Zn:0,1 Col.:0 Hsr.:0

Quantity of ingredients:
Green tea 1 teaspoon / 2g. (yes)
Water 1 cup / 120g. (yes)

Cooking instructions:
For each cup you use a teaspoonful or a teabag.
Pour green tea only with 60 to 80 ° C / 140 to 176 °F hot water, otherwise it will be bitter.
If the tea has a stimulating effect, let it draw for two to three minutes. It has a calming effect for a duration of five minutes (no longer, otherwise it will be bitter!).
Another method: Pour the tea leaves with about 70 ° C / 158 °F hot water and pour the water immediately again. Then just pour hot water again. The bitter substances disappear, and the tea gets a milder aroma.

9.75 Thick pea soup

Supports urination, detoxifying, dissolves stagnation, improves blood circulation, strengthens liver and kidney, strengthens immune system.
Cooking time approx. 2-3 hours
Allergens: AN
3 portions to 255g. / 123kcal. - (carb:47% / prot:53%)
100g.=48,37kcal. / protein 4,36g. fat:7,3g.
µg. - Ph:3,44 Na:0,25 Ka:7,5 Mg:1,22 Ca:1,55 Fe:0,06 Zn:0,04 Col.:0 Hsr.:5,21

Quantity of ingredients:
Peas, green 3/8 lbs - 6oz / 150g. (yes)
Water 2 1/4 cups / 550g. (yes)
Sesame oil 1 table spoon / 20g. (yes)
Onion white 1/2 piece / 25g. (yes)
Ginger fresh 1/2 teaspoon / 1g. (yes)
Ground 1/2 teaspoon / 1g. (yes)
Oat meal 1 table spoon / 15g. (yes)
Salt 1 pinch / 1g. (little)
Parsley 1 stem / 2g. (yes)

Cooking instructions:
Soak dried peas before cooking. Sauté sesame oil, onion, a little

oatmeal, ginger and cumin in a hot pot; add the peas and simmer for 2-3 hours; add salt at the end and purée with a blender; garnish with parsley.

9.76 Tomato soup

Promotes digestion, helps to digest fat, supports urination, reduces blood pressure, dissolves stagnation. Contains unsaturated fatty acids, is antioxidative.
Cooking time approx. 10 min
2 portions to 290g. / 100kcal. - (carb:42% / prot:58%)
100g.=34,66kcal. / protein 1,78g. fat:7,9g.
µg. - Ph:4,2 Na:1,2 Ka:31,36 Mg:1,99 Ca:3,85 Fe:0,07 Zn:0,04 Col.:0,01 Hsr.:1,47

Quantity of ingredients:
Olive oil 1 table spoon / 15g. (yes)
Onion white 1 piece / 60g. (yes)
Cinnamon ground 1 pinch / 1g. (yes)
Basil (fresh) 1 teaspoon / 2g. (yes)
Pepper (ground) 1 pinch / 0,5g. ()
Salt 1 pinch / 1g. (little)
Tomato 6 pieces / 250g. (yes)
Peppers powder 1 pinch / 1g. (yes)
Water 5/8 lbs - 8oz / 250g. (yes)

Cooking instructions:
Roast the onion in a pot. Salt and spices. Briefly roast. Put washed and quartered tomatoes in the pan. Stir and sauté briefly. Add a quart of water and heat till it boils. Cook for a quarter of an hour and puree.

9.77 Vegetable bowl with Provencal pistou

Promotes spleen and liver, reduces blood pressure, strengthens immune system, prevents cancer, reduces radiation damage, forcing spleen, dissolves stagnation. Relieves constipation, strengthens mother milk production.
Cooking time approx. 1 1/2 hours
Allergens: AGL
8 portions to 323,12g. / 138kcal. - (carb:75% / prot:25%)
100g.=42,67kcal. / protein 5,89g. fat:6,34g.
µg. - Ph:0,65 Na:0,64 Ka:2,48 Mg:1,06 Ca:4,28 Fe:0,02 Zn:0 Col.:0,01 Hsr.:0,25

Quantity of ingredients:
Tomato 5/8 oz / 200g. (yes)
Olive oil 2 table spoons / 30g. (yes)

Garlic 1 clove / 5g. (yes)
Toast bread (whole grain) 1 slice / 5g. (yes)
Parmesan 1 oz / 30g. (little)
Basil (fresh) 1 Bunch / 125g. (yes)
Salt 1 pinch / 2g. (little)
Pepper (ground) 1 pinch / 1g. ()
Oregano dried 1 teaspoon / 3g. (yes)
Basic recipe for a vegetable soup (nutritious) 3 lbs / 1250g. (yes)
Carrot 3/8 lbs - 6oz / 150g. (yes)
Celery root 1/4 lbs - 4oz / 100g. (yes)
Broccoli 5/8 oz / 200g. (yes)
Fennel 1 piece / 250g. (yes)
Thyme dried 1/2 teaspoon / 2g. (yes)
Oregano dried 1/2 teaspoon / 2g. (yes)
Bay leaf 1 piece / 0,5g. (yes)
Peas, green 1/8 lbs - 2oz / 50g. (yes)
Onion (spring onion) 4 pieces / 80g. (yes)
Potato 1/4 lbs - 4oz / 100g. (rec.)

Cooking instructions:
Sauce:
Tear off tomatoes and cut into small pieces. Reduce in a pot with a little olive oil, finely chopped garlic. Add 1 slice of dry toasted bread (crumbed), fresh finely grated Parmesan, finely chopped basil, oregano, salt and pepper.

Soup:
Boil the vegetable broth according to the basic recipe, add coarsely sliced carrots, diced celery, diced potatoes, small florets, broccoli, finely chopped fennel tuber, peas, thyme, oregano and the bay leaf. let cook 10 minutes.

Cut 4 scallions into thin rings, add them and cook another 2 min.

Pour sauce into a soup bowl. First only a few tablespoons. Stir boiling broth with it, then stir in the soup little by little.

9.78 Vegetable juice

Promotes digestion, helps to digest fat, supports urination, reduces blood pressure, strengthens immune system, prevents cancer, reduces radiation damage, forcing spleen, is stimulating.
Cooking time approx. 15 min

Allergens: L
1 portion to 225g. / 64kcal. - (carb:82% / prot:18%)
100g.=28,44kcal. / protein 2,46g. fat:0,44g.
µg. - Ph:33,92 Na:30,92 Ka:205,63 Mg:13,57 Ca:34,59 Fe:1,17 Zn:0,33 Col.:0 Hsr.:19,76

Quantity of ingredients:
Celery root 1/2 oz / 20g. (yes)
Carrot 1/4 lbs - 4oz / 100g. (yes)
Tomato 1/4 lbs - 4oz / 100g. (yes)
Garlic 1 piece / 2g. (yes)
Salt 1 teaspoon / 2g. (little)
Acerola fruit nectar or powder 1/2 teaspoon / 1g. (yes)

Cooking instructions:
Peel all ingredients and use the juicer to make a drink. Stir in the acerola.

9.79 Vegetable miso soup with tofu

Very powerful, strengthens after febrile illness, reduces blood pressure, strengthens immune system, prevents cancer, reduces radiation damage, improves blood circulation, strengthens liver and kidney, detoxifying, strengthens the muscles, reduces flatulence, forcing spleen.
Cooking time approx. 15 min
Allergens: EN
4 portions to 247,75g. / 107kcal. - (carb:22% / prot:78%)
100g.=43,09kcal. / protein 1,85g. fat:9,4g.
µg. - Ph:3,92 Na:13,88 Ka:10,98 Mg:1,98 Ca:4,08 Fe:0,07 Zn:0,01 Col.:0 Hsr.:1,45

Quantity of ingredients:
Sesame oil 2 table spoons / 35g. (yes)
Onion (shallot) 1 piece / 20g. (yes)
Carrot 1 piece / 70g. (yes)
Leek 2 inches / 10g. (yes)
Water 3 cups / 750g. (yes)
Endive salad 2 table spoons / 30g. (yes)
Soy Tofu 2 table spoons / 30g. (little)
Ginger fresh 1/2 teaspoon / 1g. (yes)
Miso 2 table spoons / 15g. (little)

Cooking instructions:
In sesame oil first sauté onions, then carrots and a little leek; Pour in water and simmer gently; add the bean sprouts and endive leaves and

leave to stand; Tofu cubes, add a little ginger; at the end stir in a little cooled cooking-water the Miso.

9.80 Vegetable rice

Forcing spleen, dissolves stagnation, promotes weight loss. Good to fight immunodeficiency, loss of appetite, flatulence, high blood pressure, strengthens kidney and bladder. Diuretic, warming the body from the inside, regulates internal organs functions.
Cooking time approx. 30 min
Allergens: L
3 portions to 274,67g. / 304kcal. - (carb:88% / prot:12%)
100g.=110,56kcal. / protein 8,1g. fat:3,4g.
µg. - Ph:11,8 Na:1,92 Ka:15,55 Mg:11,36 Ca:27,38 Fe:0,16 Zn:0,07 Col.:0 Hsr.:5,17

Quantity of ingredients:
Broccoli 1/8 lbs - 2oz / 50g. (yes)
Carrot 1/8 lbs - 2oz / 50g. (yes)
Kohlrabi 1/8 lbs - 2oz / 50g. (yes)
Cauliflower 1 oz / 30g. (yes)
Peas 1/2 oz / 20g. (yes)
Margarine 1 teaspoon / 4g. (little)
Basic recipe for a vegetable soup (nutritious) 7/8 lbs / 400g. (yes)
Parsley 1/2 oz / 20g. (yes)
Pepper (ground) 1 pinch / 0,2g. ()

Cooking instructions:
Cut the broccoli, carrots and kohlrabi into small cubes, divide the cauliflower into small florets. Heat the margarine in a pan or saucepan, sauté the vegetables. Then add the rice, top up with the vegetable stock and leave to soak for 15-20 minutes.

In the meantime, finely chop the parsley. After cooking, season the rice with freshly ground pepper and parsley.

9.81 Vitamin drink

Regulates gastrointestinal function, promotes spleen and liver, reduces blood pressure, strengthens immune system, prevents cancer, reduces radiation damage, supports urination, quenches thirst, calms the stomach, prevents cancer.
Cooking time approx. 5 min
3 portions to 273,33g. / 172kcal. - (carb:92% / prot:8%)
100g.=62,93kcal. / protein 2,78g. fat:0,57g.
µg. - Ph:9,44 Na:2,63 Ka:80,69 Mg:7,39 Ca:10,06 Fe:0,28 Zn:0,03 Col.:0 Hsr.:6,17

Quantity of ingredients:
Orange juice 1 cup / 300g. (yes)
Carrot 5/8 oz / 200g. (yes)
Banana 2 pieces / 300g. (yes)
Kiwi 1 piece / 20g. (yes)

Cooking instructions:
Chop oranges, carrots, bananas and kiwi and finely puree with the blender.

9.82 Warming carrot soup

Strengthens and warms, reduces blood pressure, strengthens immune system, prevents cancer, reduces radiation damage, strengthens gastrointestinal function.
Cooking time approx. 30 min
Allergens: HL
3 portions to 274,67g. / 133kcal. - (carb:79% / prot:21%)
100g.=48,54kcal. / protein 2,16g. fat:7,86g.
µg. - Ph:2,86 Na:2,31 Ka:9,18 Mg:8,37 Ca:32,64 Fe:0,13 Zn:0,03 Col.:0 Hsr.:1

Quantity of ingredients:
Carrot 4 pieces / 250g. (yes)
Walnut oil 2 table spoons / 20g. (yes)
Onion (shallot) 2 pieces / 40g. (yes)
Anise (Common Fennel) 1/2 teaspoon / 1g. (yes)
Nutmeg 1 pinch / 1g. (yes)
Ginger fresh 1/2 teaspoon / 1g. (yes)
Salt 1 pinch / 1g. (little)
Basic recipe for a vegetable soup (nutritious) 2 cup / 500g. (yes)
Parsley 1 table spoon / 10g. (yes)

Cooking instructions:
Heat walnut oil in a hot pot and fry onions; steam the carrots in it; add anise, nutmeg, a little ginger, salt and sauté everything; add water or vegetable- or meat stock; cook everything soft and then puree; fold in parsley at the end.

Recommendation: Suitable for the cold season, especially if you use meat broth as a liquid for infusion.

9.83 Wheat semolina with olives-herb-sauce and salad

Protects the digestive system. Detoxifying, affects anorexia, good to fight flatulence, inflammatory bowel disease, obesity, gout, stomach ulcers, stomach cramps, rheumatism, heartburn. Dissolves stagnation, relieves fatigue.
Cooking time approx. 15 min
Allergens: ACGL
3 portions to 291g. / 245kcal. - (carb:77% / prot:23%)
100g.=84,08kcal. / protein 7,65g. fat:9,46g.
µg. - Ph:4,44 Na:2,51 Ka:6,39 Mg:7,97 Ca:30,53 Fe:0,1 Zn:0,04 Col.:3,02 Hsr.:2,72

Quantity of ingredients:
Cream, sweet 30% 1/8 lbs - 2oz / 40g. (little)
Water 1/3 cup / 65g. (yes)
Wheat semolina 1/4 lbs - 4oz / 100g. (yes)
Chicken egg 1 piece / 60g. (little)
Pepper (ground) 1 pinch / 0,5g. ()
Lemon peel 1 pinch / 1g. (yes)
Onion white 1 piece / 60g. (yes)
Olive oil 1 teaspoon / 2g. (yes)
Chives 1 table spoon / 7g. (yes)
Basic recipe for a vegetable soup (nutritious) 2 cups / 500g. (yes)
Lettuce 2 handful / 30g. (yes)
Olive oil 1 teaspoon / 3g. (yes)
Lemon juice 1 teaspoon / 3g. (yes)
Oregano fresh 1 teaspoon / 2g. (yes)

Cooking instructions:
Mix cream and water and heat till it boils. Stir in the wheat semolina and cook to a thick porridge and remove from heat. Whisk the egg and stir in, season with pepper and grated lemon zest. Form with 2 coffee spoons, dumplings and leave to stir in the slightly boiling vegetable stock until the dumplings float up.
Chop the onion and roast it in olive oil in a pan. Pour the semolina dumplings into the pan and sprinkle with finely chopped chives.

Wash salad and cut into thin strips. Season with olive oil, lemon juice and oregano.

9.84 Zucchini semolina cream soup

Good to fight loss of appetite, reduces blood pressure, promotes weight loss. Good to fight loss of appetite, flatulence, inflammatory bowel

disease, rheumatism, heartburn.
Cooking time approx. 25 min
Allergens: AGL
4 portions to 341,75g. / 146kcal. - (carb:78% / prot:22%)
100g.=42,72kcal. / protein 4,02g. fat:7,8g.
µg. - Ph:1,7 Na:0,83 Ka:9,09 Mg:4,88 Ca:18,35 Fe:0,08 Zn:0,02 Col.:0,22 Hsr.:0,82

Quantity of ingredients:
Butter organic 1/2 oz / 20g. (little)
Wheat semolina 2 table spoons / 20g. (yes)
Parsley 1 Bunch / 100g. (yes)
Basic recipe for a vegetable soup (nutritious) 3 1/2 cups / 800g. (yes)
Lovage 1/2 teaspoon / 2g. (yes)
Nutmeg 1 pinch / 0,5g. (yes)
Anise (Common Fennel) 1 pinch / 0,5g. (yes)
Zucchini 7/8 lbs / 400g. (yes)
Ginger fresh 1/2 teaspoon / 1g. (yes)
Crème fraiche cheese 2 table spoons / 20g. (little)
Lemon peel 1/4 piece / 2g. (yes)
Salt 1 pinch / 1g. (little)
Pepper (ground) 1 pinch / 0,5g. ()

Cooking instructions:
Melt the butter in a saucepan, add the semolina and fry briefly while stirring. Add half of the chopped parsley, sauté for a short time, pour vegetable broth according to the basic recipe, season with chopped lovage, nutmeg and anise. Cook the soup without lid lightly for 10 minutes. Add the finely chopped zucchini and the small piece of lemon zest, cook gently for 5 minutes until the zucchini are tender. Remove the lemon peel.
Using the blender, finely puree the soup with the crème fraiche and the remaining parsley.

10 Effects of food

10.1 Use ingredients: recommendable

Acai powder
Bitter Herb liqueur
Cream 10% coffee cream
Cucumber (spicy cucumber)
Fox nut, gorgon nut, makhana
Hibiscus

Kudzu
Lily bulbs
Mascarpone cheese
Potato
Potato (mealy)
Salmon

10.2 Use ingredients: yes

Acerola fruit nectar or powder
Agar agar (kelp)
Agave nectar
Agrimony
Almond
Almond milk
Almond puree
Aloe juice
Amaranth
Amaranth Pops
Angelica root
Anise (Common Fennel)
Apple (sour)
Apple (sweet)
Apple juice (natural cloudy)
Apple puree
Apricot
Apricot dried
Apricot jam
Apricot nectar
Apricots
Apricots juice
Arrowroot
Artichoke
Asparagus (green or white)
Aubergine
Avocado
Balm
Bamboo shoots
Banana
Banana (cooking banana)
Banchatee (green tea)
barberry
Barley
Barley flour
Barley grass powder
Barley grouts
Barley malt
Barley not peeled
Basic recipe for a beef soup

Basic recipe for a beef soup (warming)
Basic recipe for a chicken soup
(warming)
Basic recipe for a duck soup
Basic recipe for a fish soup
Basic recipe for a rice soup (Congee)
Basic recipe for a vegetable soup
(nutritious)
Basil
Basil (fresh)
Batavia
Bay leaf
Bean oil
Bearberry leaf
Berries of the season
Berry juice
Bitter Lemon
Bitter orange peel
Black caraway
Black fungus mushroom
Black tea
Blackberry dried (unripe fruit)
Blackberry jam
Blackberry leaves
Blackberry´s
Blackthorn (Sloe)
Blue mallow tee
Blueberry
Blueberry dried
Blueberry jam
Blueberry juice
Bocksdorn fruits (Fructus Lycii, Goji,
goji berry dried
Boletus mushroom
Borage
Borage oil
Boxhorn clover seeds
Bread roll
Bread with carob kernel flour
Breadcrumbs (wheat bread, bread roll)

Broccoli
Brussels sprouts
Buckbean
Buckwheat
Buckwheat (roasted) Kasha
Buckwheat whole grain
Bulgur (cereals)
Burdock root tea
Buttermilk
Cantaloupe
Carambola (Star fruit)
Cardamom
Carob flour, St. john's bread
Carrot
Carrot (Early Carrot)
Carrot juice without sugar
Cashews
Cauliflower
Celery root
Celery sticks
Cereal coffee
Chamomile
Chamomile tea
Champignon
Channa-Dal
Chanterelle
Chard
Chenpi (chinese tangerine bowl)
Cherry
Cherry (sour)
Cherry compote
Cherry juice
Chervil
Chervil dried
Chestnut puree
Chestnuts
Chickpeas
Chickweed
Chicory
Chili (pod or ground)
Chinese cabbage
Chinese pearl barley
Chives
Chlorella (fresh water)
Chocolate
Chocolate (Diabetic)
Chrysanthemum blossom tea
Cinnamon ground
Cinnamon sticks
Clementine
Clementines
Clove
Cocoa
Coconut flakes

Coconut grated
Coconut meat
Coconut milk
Coix (seeds) YiYi Ren
Cola drink
Cola drink (low calorie)
Compote (fruits of the season)
Coriander
Coriander (fresh)
Corn
Corn (fast polenta)
Corn (roasted)
Corn flour
Corn germ oil
Corn Grease (Polenta)
Corn silk tea
Corn starch
Couscous
Cow's milk (1.5% fat)
Cow's milk (whole milk 3.5% fat)
Cranberries
Cranberry
Cranberry
Cranberry jam
Cranberry juice
Cress
Crispbread
Crucian
Cucumber
Cucumber (bitter)
Cumin (Caraway seed)
Curcuma
Currant (black)
Currant (red)
Currant (white)
Currant jam (black)
Currant jam (red)
Currant juice (black)
Currants (black)
Currants (red)
Curry
Curry paste red
Daisy
Dandelion (young plants)
Dandelion juice
Dandelionroots tea
Dashi
Dates dried
Dates red
Dill
Dulse (seaweed)
Dyer's broom herb
Elderberries
Elderberry blossom tee

Endive salad
Evening primrose oil
Fennel
Fennel seeds ground
Fennel tea
Fenugreek (Trigonella foenum-graecum)
Fig
Fig dried
Flower pollen
Fructose (glucose)
Fruit mix juice
Fruit tea
Gail plum
Galangal
Garam Masala powder
Garlic
Gelee Royal
Gentian root
Gentian root tea
Ginger fresh
Ginger oil
Ginger powder
Ginkgo fruit
Ginseng
Ginseng root
Gooseberry
Gourd
Grape juice red
Grape juice white
Grapefruit (Pomelo)
Grapefruit dried peel
Grapefruit juice
Grapes red
Grapes white
Grapeseed oil
Green spelt
Green tea
Greengage
Ground
Ground caraway
Guava
Hawthorn
Hazelnuts
Herbal tea mix
Herbs bitter
Herbs of Provence
Herbs various
Herbs wild
Hibiscus tea
Hijiki
Hokkaido pumpkin
Honey
Hop

Horehound leaves
Hyssop
Iceberg lettuce
Jasmine blossoms tee
Juniper berry
Kaki plum
Kalmus
King Solomon's-seal
Kiwi
Kohlrabi
Kombu seaweed (Saccharina japonica)
Kukicha tea
Kumquats
Lamb's lettuce
Lamb's lettuce
Lavender blossoms
Leaf salads (bitter)
Leek
Lemon
Lemon Balm (dried)
Lemon Balm (fresh)
Lemon juice
Lemon peel
Lemongrass
Lettuce
Licorice root tea
Lime
Lime blossom tea
Linseed
Linseed (crushed)
Linseed oil
Liver smoothing tea
Longane
Loquate / Japanese medlar
Lotus roots
Lotus seeds
Lovage
Lovage seeds
Luo Han Guo fruit
Lychee
Lychee in Preserved
Lye roll
Mallow (Malva sylvestris) blossom tea
Malt
Mango
Mango juice
Manioc flour
Maple syrup
Mare's milk
Marjoram
Medlar
Millet
Millet flakes
Mirabelle plum

Morel (black, dried)
Morel, dried
Mozzarella
Mu Erh Mushroom
Muesli
Mulberry fruit
Mulled Wine Spice
Mullet
Multi-grain bread (gray bread)
Mung bean
Mung bean sprouting
Mustard
Mustard Dijon
Mustard medium hot
Mustard seeds
Mustard sweet
Nasturtium (nose-twister or nose-tweaker)
Nectarine
Nettles
Nutmeg
Oat
Oat flakes (whole grain)
Oat flakes roasted
Oat flour
Oat fusion (baby food)
Oat meal
Oat milk
Okra
Olive oil
Olives
Olives green
Onion (shallot)
Onion (spring onion)
Onion read
Onion white
Orange
Orange blossom
Orange dried peel
Orange grated peel
Orange jam
Orange juice
Orange peel
Oregano dried
Oregano fresh
Oyster mushroom
Oyster shell powder
Palm oil
Papaya
Parsley
Parsley root
Parsnip
Passion blossoms tea
Passion fruit

Peaches
Peaches (canned)
Pear
Pear juice
Pearl barley
Pearl barley
Peas
Peas, green
Pepper (ground)
Pepper Cayenne
Pepper powder (hot)
Pepper white (ground)
Peppercorns
Peppermint
Peppermint tea
Pepperoni
Pepperoni, red, pitted, halved
Pepperoni, yellow, pitted, halved
Peppers
Peppers (rose peppers)
Peppers (sweet)
Peppers powder
Pickle
Pimento
Pine nuts
Pineapple
Pineapple juice without sugar
Pistachios
Plum
Plum dried
Plums
Pomegranate
Poppy
Potato flour
Prickly pear
Psyllium seed
Pudding powder vanilla
Pumpernickel (dark bread)
Pumpkin
Pumpkin seed oil
Pumpkin seeds
Quince
Quinoa
Radicchio
Radish
Radish (white, green, purple-red)
Radish black
Radish horseradish
Radish leaves
Raisins
Rapeseed oil
Raspberry
Raspberry dried (immature)
Raspberry jam

Raspberry leaf tea
Red beet
Red berry (without sugar)
Red cabbage
Reishi mushroom
Rhubarb
Ribworttea
Rice (fragrance)
Rice (Gaoliang / Sorghum)
Rice (whole grain)
Rice Basmati
Rice black
Rice long grain rice
Rice malt
Rice noodles
Rice red
Rice round grain
Rice starch
Rice sticky
Rice sweet
Rice variety any
Rice wild (nature rice)
Romaine lettuce / lettuce salad
Rose blossom tea
Rose hip
Rose hip tea
Rose leaf tea
Rosemary
Rucola
Rusk
Rye
Rye flour
Rye wholemeal bread
Safflower (Dyer's thistle / Hong Hua)
Saffron
Sage
Sago (cereals)
Sake
Salsify
Sauerkraut (cutted cabbage fermented)
Savory
Savoy cabbage / kale
Sea buckthorn
Sea cucumber
Seacrab
Sesame oil
Sesame oil roasted
Sesame paste (Tahini)
Sesame, black
Sesame, white
Shark
Shiitake, dried
Slug
Sorrel

Sour cherries
Sourdough
Spelled (Dark) bread
Spelled flakes
Spelled grain
Spelled semolina
Spelled wholemeal flour
Spinach
St. Benedict's thistle, blessed thistle,
holy thistle, spotted thistle
Star anise
Stevia (candyleaf, sweetleaf)
Strawberries
Strawberry jam
Strawberry Juice
Sugar - icing sugar
Sugar brown
Sugar candy white
Sugar cane sugar
Sugar fructose - fruit sugar
Sugar glucose - grapes sugar
Sugar Milk Sugar
Sugar molasses
Sugar palm sugar
Sugar substitute (sweetener)
Sugar white
Sunflower oil
Sunflower seeds
Sweet potato
Tangerine
Tarragon (Estragon)
Tea mixture uric acid lowering
Thistle oil
Thyme
Thyme dried
Toast bread (whole grain)
Tomato
Tomato dried
Tomato juice
Tomato paste
Tomato puree
Tonic Water
Topinambur
Truffle
Tsampa (roasted barley flour)
Turmeric (yellow root)
Turnip
Turnips
Umeboshi paste
Umeboshi plums (Japanese apricots)
Valerian
Vanilla
Vanilla pod
Vanilla powder

Vanilla sugar natural
Vegetable juice
Vinegar (Apple vinegar)
Vinegar (Red wine vinegar)
Vinegar Aceto Balsamico
Vinegar Aceto Balsamico white
Wakame
Walnut oil
Walnuts
Walnuts roasted
Water
Water hot
Watermelon
Wax gourd
Wheat
Wheat bran
Wheat bulgur
Wheat flakes
Wheat flatbread/pita bread
Wheat flour
Wheat flour whole grain
Wheat germ oil
Wheat semolina
Wheat semolina for children
Wheat/Rye/Gray-black bread with yeast
Wheatgrass juice

Wheatgrass powder
Whey
White bread (baguette)
White bread (pretzel sticks)
White bread (roll)
White bread (wheat bread)
White breadcrumbs
White cabbage
White dumpling bread (wheat bread cut into chunks)
Whole grain bread
Wholemeal flour
Wild garlic (garlic spinach)
Wild herbs
Wild strawberries
Wormwood herb
Yam root, yam root tuber
Yarrow
Yarrow tea
Yeast
Yew nut
Yoghurt vanilla
Yogi tea
Yogurt (natural, 1.5% fat)
Yogurt (natural, 3.5% fat)
Zucchini

10.3 Use ingredients: little

Adzuki beans
Almond marzipan
Anchovy / Sardine
Baking powder
Beans (green, fresh)
Beef bone marrow
Beef fillet
Beef heart
Beef heart (calf)
Beef kidney
Beef liver
Beef lungs (calf)
Beef meat
Beef meat (calf)
Beef meatbones
Beef Oxtail pieces
Beef soup meat
Beef stomach
Beer (alcohol-free)
Bitter liqueur
Black beans
Black-eyed peas
Brazil nuts
Brie cheese

Broad beans (thick beans)
Brown ale
Bush beans
Butter (half fat)
Butter beans white
Butter Bio
Calamari
Camembert
Campari
Carp
Caviar
Chicken Blood
Chicken egg
Chicken egg white
Chicken heart
Chicken liver
Chicken meat
Chicken stomach
Chicken yolk
Cod
Codfish
Coffee
Cooking oil
Cottage cheese

Crab
Cream (30% fat)
Cream sour 10%
Cream sour 20%
Cream sour 30%
Cream, sweet 30%
Creamer
Creme fraiche cheese
Curd cheese 20%
Curd cheese 40%
Deer meat
Deer meat
Deer's Bones
Deer's kidneys
Duck (heart)
Duck (slaughtered)
Ducks egg
Edam cheese
Eel
Eel smoked
Emmental cheese
Fernet Branca (herbal bitter liqueur)
Feta cheese
Fish innards
Fish pieces mixed (fresh water)
Fish remains
Fish sauce
Flounder
French beans
Fresh cheese
Fresh cheese from soya
Fresh cheese with herbs
Freshwater crab
Freshwater fish
Gelatin white
Ginseng liqueur
Goat
Goat and sheep's blood
Goat and sheep's brain
Goat and sheep's liver
Goat and sheep's milk
Goat and sheep's stomach
Goat cheese
Goose
Goose blood
Goose egg
Goose fat
Goose parts
Gorgonzola
Gouda cheese
Grass carp
Halibut (Flatfish)
Herring
Honey wine (Met)

Horse meat
Jellyfish
Kefir
Kidney beans (red)
Ladyfingers
Lamb bones
Lamb kidneys
Lamb liver
Lamb meat
Lamb shoulder
Lentils
Lentils black
Lentils red
Lentils yellow
Lima beans
Lobster
Lychee liqueur
Mackerel
Margarine
Margarine (diet)
Martini
Mayonnaise 50%
Mayonnaise 80%
Mediterranean fish (cod, plaice,
haddock, sea eel, mackerel)
Mineral water
Miso
Miso black (fermented)
Miso paste (soy bean paste)
Mixed Pickles
Mold cheese
Mussels
Mutton
Mutton
Noodles (wheat) with egg
Noodles (wheat, lasagne) with egg
Noodles (wheat, ribbon noodles) with
egg
Noodles (wheat, spaghetti) with egg
Noodles (whole grain) with egg
Nori, purple seaweed, red algae
Octopus
Octopus
Oysters
Parmesan
Peanut (roasted)
Peanut oil
Peanuts
Perch
Pheasant
Pig blood
Pigeon
Pigeon egg
Pineapple (from a can)

Pinto beans speckled
Plaice
Pork Bacon
Pork brain
Pork fat (lard)
Pork ham
Pork ham cooked
Pork ham smoked
Pork heart
Pork kidneys
Pork knuckle
Pork liver
Pork lung
Pork marrow bones
Pork meat
Pork skin
Pork stomach
Pork/beef sausage (smoked)
Pork's intestine
Processed cheese 12%
processed cheese 30%
Puff pastry
Quail
Quail egg
Rabbit
Rabbit (wild)
Rabbit liver
Rabbit meat
Rice flour
Rice mash
Rosefish
Salt

Salt (herbal)
Sheep's milk
Sheep's milk yoghurt
Shrimp
Shrimps
Skim milk powder
Sour cream 15% fat
Sour milk
Sour milk cheese 20%
Soy flour
Soy noodles
Soy Tofu
Soy Tofu smoked
Soya Cuisine (soy cream)
Soybean milk
Soybean oil
Soybeans
Soybeans, black
Soybeans, blacks, fermented
Soybeans, yellow
Spiny lobsters
Spurdog (spiny dogfish, Schillerlocken)
Tabasco
Trout
Trout (smoked)
Tuna
Turkey breast meat
Turkey ham
White beans
Whitefish
Wild boar meat

10.4 Do not use contra-acting foods

Beer (alcohol-reduced)
Beer (Pils)
Beer (Top-fermented German dark beer)
Capers in olive oil
Clarified butter
Coconut fat
Feta cheese
Peanut butter
Pork Lard
Pork sausage (Bratwurst)

Prosecco
Red wine
Rum
Sherry (whine)
Soy sauce
Spirit
Supplementary nutrition
Wheat beer
White wine
Wormwood

11 Complementary

11.1 Corn silk

Zea mays, stigmata
Preparation: Healing tea (infusion)
Supports urination, relaxes the veins, reduces blood sugar.
Dosage: 10-30 g

11.2 Valerian

Valerian has a soothing, astringent and astringent effect, cramping and muscle relaxing. He also mentally has a slightly stimulating effect. Through these effects he is able to influence inner unrest, anxiety and tension.

11.3 Nettles

Promotes urination. Tea or juice, cleanses the blood and the kidneys, supports prostate problems, inhibit the formation of inflammation, pain-relieving.

11.4 Dill

The medicinal and spice herb has an antispasmodic effect and stimulates gastric juice production. Good to fight flatulence. Antispasmodic for gastrointestinal discomfort.

11.5 Chamomile

Antispasmodic and anti-inflammatory for digestive disorders, soothes the nerves and promotes good sleep. Applied externally, it heals wounds in the mouth-throat area and the skin. Strengthens eyesight.

11.6 Chervil dried

Forces urination, detoxifying, blood-purifying and blood-pressure-reducing effects.

11.7 Coriander

The essential oils are appetizing, digestive, cramping and soothing in stomach and intestinal disorders.

11.8 Lovage

Stimulates digestion, reduces pain. Extracts of the root are used to flush out urinary tract infections and prevent kidney gravel.

11.9 Dandelion (young plants)

Detoxifies, relieves inflammation. Regulates digestion, helps with rheumatism, releases kidney stones, leaves pimples and chronic skin disorders disappear.

11.10   Parsley

Stimulates liver function, detoxifies. Forces urinating. Relieves flatulence. Digestive and menstrual stimulating, birth-accelerating, memory-enhancing, blood-purifying, skin-smoothing.

11.11   Peppermint

Relaxes, frees the lungs and the nose (inhale), regulates the cycle. Stimulates bile flow and bile production, antispasmodic in gastrointestinal disorders, antimicrobial and antiviral.

11.12   Rosemary

Promotes digestion, relieves bloating, strengthens lung, spleen and kidney. Affects the circulation and nerves. Appetizing. Baths help to fight circulatory disorders as well as with gout and rheumatism.

11.13   Black caraway

Detoxifying, immunoregulatory. In addition, the oil should stimulate the formation of bone marrow cells and generally protect body cells from viruses.

11.14   Thyme dried

Disinfecting. It stimulates the blood circulation, increases the appetite and helps to digest fat meat better. Strengthens lungs and spleen (TCM).

12 Basics of Nutrition

The basic principles of nutrition described herein are general recommendations. They are not aimed at a specific form of therapy. Recommendations concerning a therapy have priority.

12.1 Nutrition

Regular meals in a relaxed atmosphere. A warm breakfast is considered a good start into the day.
The main meals ought to be taken for lunch – supper in the early evening. Pay attention to feeling hungry or sated: don't eat too much nor remain hungry is the rule
Prepare the meals freshly from natural, regional products. Frozen, heat-conserved, industrially prepared or foodstuffs cooked in the microwave oven are rejected.
Choice of foodstuffs according to the season: more cooling food in summer, more warming food in winter.
Eat cooked food at least twice a day. Food and drinks ought to be lukewarm, never ice-cold or hot.
Raw vegetables, briefly cooked vegetables, freshly squeezed juices and mineral water are not recommended. Milk and dairy products are only included in the diet if they don't cause problems.
Don't use therapeutic recipes over a longer period without consulting your doctor or therapist.

Varied food
Enjoy the diversity of foodstuffs. Characteristics of a balanced nutrition are variety, suitable combination and a balanced quantity of rich and low energy foodstuffs (on one hand avoiding undersupply with essential nutrients and on the other hand to take to many undesirable substances).

A lot of Cereal Products - and Potatoes
Bread, pasta, rice, cereal flakes (best wholemeal) as well as potatoes contain almost no fat, but many vitamins, mineral nutrients, trace elements, roughage and secondary plant substances. These foodstuffs ought to be taken with low-fat side dishes.

Vegetables and Fruit – „Take Five" every day …
5 portions of vegetables and fruit a day, as fresh as possible, briefly cooked, or maybe one portion as a juice – ideal as a side dish to every meal as well as snack between meals: Thus a lot of vitamins, mineral nutrients as well as roughage and secondary plant substances

Daily milk and dairy products
Milk and Dairy Products every Day, once or twice per Week Fish; meat, sausages as well as eggs moderately. These foodstuffs contain valuable nutrients like calcium in the milk, iodine selenium and omega-3 fat acids in saltwater fish. Meat is favorable due to its high content of disposable iron and the vitamins B1, B6 and B12. Quantities of 300 – 600 g meat and sausage per week are sufficient. Prefer low-fat products, especially in meat- and dairy products.

Low-fat and fatty Foodstuffs
Fat supplies us with essential fat acids and fatty foodstuffs contain also fat-soluble vitamins. Fat is high in energy; therefore much fat in the food may cause overweight, possibly also cancer. Too many saturated fat acids may further a tendency for cardio-vascular diseases in the long term. Prefer vegetable oils and fats (e.g. rapeseed-, olive-, soya-oils and solid fats produced therefrom). Beware of invisible fat in meat- and dairy products, pastry and sweets as well as in fast-food and convenience foods. 70 – 90 g fat per day is sufficient.

Moderately Sugar and Salt
Take sugar and foods/drinks containing various kinds of sugar (e.g. glucose syrup) only occasionally. Use herbs and spices as well as a little salt creatively. Prefer salt containing iodine.

Plenty of Liquids
Water is absolutely essential. Drink 1-2 l liquids every day. Prefer water (with or without gas) and other low-calorie drinks. Alcoholic drinks should not be taken.

Tasty Dishes, carefully cooked
Cook the meals with as low temperatures and as short as possible, using little water and fat – this preserves the original taste, keeps the nutrients intact and prevents the production of harmful compounds.

Take time and enjoy the food
Take your Time and enjoy your Food
Eating consciously helps to eat right. The eye enjoys food, too. It's fun, invites to enjoy varied dishes and stimulates the feeling of satiety.

Watch your Weight and stay in Motion
A balanced diet and a lot of exercise and sport (30 – 60 min/day) are a healthy combination. The right weight furthers well-being and health. Thermals, directional effectiveness, digestive power

There are various criteria for judging the effectiveness of herbs and foodstuffs.

The use of certain herbs and ingredients is based on observations of the effects on the body which these foodstuffs, herbs and spices show after having eaten them. The medical science has developed following system: Every ingredient or herb has a directional effectiveness. Furthermore, there are herbs which have a special effect on certain organs.

The basic condition for a healthy metabolism is to obtain sufficient energy from food and that the digestive process doesn't use too much energy. An easily digestible meal makes content and sated, doesn't cause flatulence and fatigue after the meal. The perfect spices increase the healthiness of our meals. Very often, just small doses of herbs and spices will suffice. They are not used to make us sated, but to help our digestive organs to digest the food.

12.2 Recipes

The recipes list the ingredients to be used and the
Cooking instructions show how the dish is prepared. The list of ingredients shows the concerned quantities as well as the relevance for the therapy. If you find „less than mentioned", try to comply or find an alternative from the „list of recommended foodstuffs". Mostly it shall result just in a small change of taste when you simply avoid this ingredient.
Mild cooking methods: boiling, stewing, poaching, steaming
Strong cooking methods: barbecuing, roasting, frying, smoking
Balanced cooking methods: deep-frying, baking brick
Deep-freezing and warming in the microwave oven should be avoided (denaturalization).

12.3 Foodstuffs

Foodstuffs have an effect on body and soul like medicinal herbs, only a very much milder one. Dietary advice is mainly based on regional foodstuffs. The knowledge about the effects of each foodstuff and the knowledge, when which foodstuff shall be used, is based on the orthodox school of medicine. Use ecologic-organic products, if possible. As everything should be cooked for a long time due to a better digestability and very rarely eaten raw, the food agrees with everyone.

The classification of the foodstuffs according to their effect on the body is the basis in order to achieve a harmonious status of health.

Dietary advisors do not recommend certain foodstuffs for everyone. The individual diet is tailor-made for the individual constitution.

Buy only fresh and ripe fruit and vegetables. You ought to leave unripe fruit and vegetables and such with brown spots and wilted leaves behind in the market. In this case take deep-frozen goods (never ready-to-serve dishes!). Fruit and vegetables are deep-frozen immediately after harvesting and often contain more vitamins and minerals than the goods from the vegetable shelf. Whereas conserved or tinned goods contain very much less biological substances. Also, salt, sugar and others are mostly added to the latter. Never leave the foodstuffs in the water after washing them to avoid that many vital substances get drowned. Clean salads, fruit and vegetables immediately before serving.

Please make sure of the hygienic processing of foodstuffs. Clean your salads, fruit and vegetables carefully. When cooking with meat, prepare all ingredients first and then process the meat products. Clean the worktop and tools very carefully. Wooden surfaces ought to be treated with a mild disinfectant regularly in order to reduce germination.

Store fruit and vegetables separately, if possible. Harvested fruit and vegetables are still alive and emit e.g. ethylene gas, which makes other products ripen and age faster. Keep meat and fish in the closed packaging or store them in the fridge in closed containers.

12.4 Herbs

There are some basic rules for storing medicinal herbs. On principle, herbs must be protected from direct sunlight, humidity and heat.

Containers for the storage of herbs may be glasses, ceramic jars and even plastic containers. However, plastic is a rather unsuitable material and should only be a short-term solution. In case of glass containers, use a dark material.

Medicinal herbs cannot be kept for any long period. The shelf life of herbs is limited. However, it can be prolonged with suitable storage. The place should be dark, rather cool and absolutely dry. A wooden medicine cabinet, placed not directly next to a source of heat, would be ideal. Never buy large quantities of herbs so as not to have to throw them away. Label the container with the name of the herb and the date of harvesting or processing.

13 Other dietic-books

The following syndromes of dietetics, TCM or for a therapy supplement for cancer are available.

Dietetics

E001. Nutrition of the infant - baby food
E002. Nutrition during lactation
E003. Nutrition in old age
E004. Nutrition of children and adolescents
E005. Nutrition of athletes
E006. Light weight
E007. Pregnancy
E008. Full food

Protein and electrolyte - kidneys
E009. (hemodialysis) dialysis treatment
E010. Acute renal failure
E011. Chronic renal insufficiency
E012. Nephrotic syndrome
E013. Kidney stones (nephrolithiasis)

Gastrointestinal tract - pancreas
E014. Acute pancreatitis (inflammation of the pancreas)
E015. Chronic pancreatitis (inflammation of the pancreas)

Gastrointestinal tract - small intestine and large intestine
E016. Acute obstipation (constipation)
E017. Chronic obstipation (constipation)
E018. Colon irritabile
E019. Diverticulitis
E020. Acquired lactose intolerance (lactose malabsorption)
E021. Fructose malabsorption
E022. Glutensensitive enteropathy (celiac disease)
E023. Colectomy
E024. Short Bowel Syndrome

Gastrointestinal tract - liver, gallbladder, bile ducts
E025. Acute and chronic hepatitis (inflammation of the liver)
E026. Cholelithiasis (bile stones)
E027. fatty liver
E028. cirrhosis

Gastrointestinal tract - Stomach and duodenal intestine
E029. Acute gastritis
E030. Chronic gastritis
E031. Stomach bleeding
E032. Ulcus ventriculi and duodenal ulcer
E033. Condition after gastric surgery

Gastrointestinal tract - oral cavity and esophagus
E034. Stomatitis
E035. Esophageal carcinoma (esophageal cancer)
E036. Refluosophagitis (heartburn)

Special diseases
E037. Phenylketonuria (PKU)
E038. Rheumatic joint diseases

Metabolism
E039. Obesity (overweight)
E040. Diabetes mellitus
E041. Eating disorders (underweight)

Fat metabolism
E042. Hypercholesterolaemia (increased cholesterol level)
E043. Hepatic Encephalopathy

Heart and circulation
E044. Arteriosclerosis (arterial calcification)
E045. Heart insufficiency
E046. Hypertension
E047. Hyperuricaemia and gout

Changed nutrient requirements
E048. In case of fever
E049. For malignant diseases
E050. After burns
E051. Radiation and chemotherapy

CANCER
E100. Pancreatic cancer
E101. Bladder cancer
E102. Blood cancer (leukemia)
E103. Breast cancer
E104. Colorectal cancer
E105. Gastric cancer
E106. Kidney cancer
E107. Esophageal cancer

TCM
E200. Bladder - moisture heat in the bladder
E201. Bladder - moisture and cold in the bladder
E202. Bladder - emptiness and cold in the bladder
E203. Large intestine - external cold affects the large intestine
E204. Large intestine - moisture heat in the large intestine
E205. Large intestine - heat blocks the intestine II acute
E206. Large intestine - dryness of the colon
E207. Large intestine - Yang deficiency (cold)
E208. Heart - Blood insufficiency
E209. Heart - Blood stagnation
E210. Heart - Fire
E211. Heart - Hot mucus clogs the heart pores

E212. Heart - Cold mucus clogs the heart pores
E213. Heart - Qi deficiency
E214. Heart - Yang deficiency
E215. Heart - Yin deficiency
E216. Liver - Ascending Liver Yang
E217. Liver - Blood deficiency
E218. Liver - Blood stagnation
E219. Liver - Moisture heat in liver and gall bladder
E220. Liver - Fire
E221. Liver - Gall bladder Qi-Empty
E222. Liver - Cold in the liver meridian
E223. Liver - Qi stagnation
E224. Liver - Wind
E225. Liver - Wind with ascending liver Yang
E226. Liver - Wind with blood anemic
E227. Liver - Wind with extreme heat
E228. Lung - Qi deficiency
E229. Lung - Mucus-moisture in the lungs
E230. Lung - Mucus-heat in the lungs
E231. Lung - Mucus-cold in the lungs
E232. Lung - Dryness of the lungs
E233. Lung - Wind-heat attacks the lungs
E234. Lung - Wind-cold affects the lungs
E235. Lung - Yin deficiency
E236. Stomach - Bloodstagnation
E237. Stomach - Fire
E238. Stomach - Cold with liquid
E239. Stomach - Nutrition stagnation
E240. Stomach - Qi deficiency
E241. Stomach - Rebellious Qi
E242. Stomach - Yin Emptiness
E243. Spleen - Heat and moisture attack the spleen
E244. Spleen - Coldness and moisture affects the spleen
E245. Spleen - Qi deficiency
E246. Spleen - Qi deficiency + Declining spleen Qi
E247. Spleen - Qi deficiency + spleen does not control the blood
E248. Spleen - Yang deficiency
E249. Kidney - Heart and kidney no longer communicate
E250. Kidney - Jing deficiency
E251. Kidney - Kidneys cannot receive the Qi
E252. Kidney - Qi is not stable
E253. Kidney - Yang deficiency
E254. Kidney - Yin deficiency

For further information visit di-book.com.

14 EBNS - Software for nutritional counseling

The main task of the database is to create personalized nutritional advice for each patient individually. The database was developed for Dietetics

and Traditional Chinese Medicine.
The Database supports training and advices in the daily work routine.

The computer program provides lists of recipes, ingredients and herbs, which are given to the client. individually adjustable according to patient's request from whole food to vegetarians (lacto, ovo, ...). For every register there is an information sheet which can be given to the client. All texts can be individually designed.

The syndromes can be combined and result in an intersection of the recommended recipes and ingredients. The automated diagnosis for the TCM enables you to check your experience during the training as well as to confirm your diagnosis in the working day. You select several predefined symptoms and have the program automatically display the relevant syndromes.

How to work with the database:
Select the patient / client, select one or more of the syndromes you diagnosed and print the folder.

You can change all values, create new symptoms or syndromes, develop recipes, change or adapt ingredients and herbs to your findings. In simple client management, all relevant data about the person is stored. You get an overview of the past diagnoses and the development of the course of the disease.

As a consultant you save a lot of time when you print out the recipe, food and herbal lists for the recognized syndromes and give them to the clients. You can use this time for a personal conversation. With the database, dieticians and nutritionists can view the nutrients and trace elements for each recipe and develop recipes for syndromes even with suggested ingredients.

All recipe and grocery lists can also be ordered from me as a combination of several diseases. I wish all readers good luck, health and happiness in life.
More information can be found at www.ebns.at.
Volunteer: www.krebsinfo.at
Josef Miligui